Praise for

JESUS DIED FOR THIS?

It has been said that the biggest obstacle to Christ has been Christians. Becky Garrison's book is a lovely reminder that Jesus has survived the embarrassing things we have done in his name, and it is an invitation not to reject Christ because of his followers — after all, we've been a mess from the beginning. And it is also a call, not just to complain about the church we see, but to become the church we dream of.

> SHANE CLAIBORNE, author, activist, and
> recovering sinner, *www.thesimpleway.org*

Becky Garrison punctures the top-heavy, celebrity-loaded monster that has become the universe of big-time American religion. This book is long overdue.

> FRANK SCHAEFFER, author of
> *Crazy for God*

Becky Garrison is, without a doubt, Christianity's premier religious satirist; and in this memoir-cum-travelogue, she takes on the foibles and failings of the faith with all the brio her readers have come to expect from her. Rarely, if ever, has irreverence been rendered more holy than it is here.

urer,

merica

D1502838

I found *Jesus Died for This?* to be a winsome book that evokes snickers and embarrassing nods — as good satire should do — and yet also reveals an urgency beneath the laughs, lacking even in many "serious" Christian books, that attempts to constructively tackle the state of the church that we have allowed to take shape. For this reason, I highly recommend it as a book about our current church and some of our most important midcourse corrections, but also as a storytelling strategy that will allow the next generation to join the conversation.

ANDREW JONES, Boaz Project,
blogger at TallSkinnyKiwi

Among Christian writers, Becky Garrison stands out as one of the most willing to respectfully and thoughtfully engage alternative views, especially those of atheists, agnostics, and even humanists like me. Religious and nonreligious readers alike should make themselves aware of her voice. With her great sense of humor, they'll be glad they did.

GREG M. EPSTEIN, humanist chaplain,
Harvard University

JESUS DIED FOR THIS?

JESUS DIED FOR THIS?

A Satirist's Search for the Risen Christ

BECKY GARRISON

ZONDERVAN®

ZONDERVAN.com/
AUTHORTRACKER
follow your favorite authors

ZONDERVAN

Jesus Died for This?
Copyright © 2010 by Becky Garrison

This title is also available as a Zondervan ebook.
Visit www.zondervan.com/ebooks.

This title is also available in a Zondervan audio edition.
Visit www.zondervan.fm.

Requests for information should be addressed to:
Zondervan, *Grand Rapids, Michigan 49530*

Library of Congress Cataloging-in-Publication Data

Garrison, Becky, 1961–
    Jesus died for this? : a satirist's search for the risen Christ / Becky Garrison.
        p.   cm.
    Includes bibliographical references.
    ISBN 978-0-310-29289-0 (softcover)
    1. Garrison, Becky, 1961– 2. Christian pilgrims and pilgrimages. 3. Christian
life. I. Title.
    BR1725.G377A3   2010
    269.092—dc22
    [B]   201001212

Cover design: John Hamilton Design
Cover photography: Robin Bartholick / Getty Images®
Interior photographs: copyright © Becky Garrison
Interior design: Beth Shagene

Printed in the United States of America

10 11 12 13 14 15 /DCI/ 21 20 19 18 17 16 15 14 13 12 11 10 9 8 7 6 5 4 3 2 1

*For our sake he was crucified under Pontius Pilate;
he suffered death and was buried.
On the third day he rose again...*
The Nicene Creed

*It's time we untangle the narrative of faith
from the fundamentalists, pious self-helpers, and
religio-profiteers. And let's do it with holy mischief
rather than ideological firepower.*
Geez magazine

*Satire has become my grail; it is the chalice I drink
from where I know God is in charge. Christ has given me
redemption, and I can laugh at my feeble attempt at trying
to do something with this fledgling faith.*
Murray Stiller, filmmaker, *Nailin' It to the Church*

Contents

The *Itinerarium*

Although I possess this inborn hunger to connect with the Jesus whom I encounter in the Gospels, I often wonder if he's truly present when Christians gather together in his name. Are we really trying to put his teachings into practice or playing the Sunday morning God game? Watching the Christian cliques gather — the holy hipsters, the Promise Keeper/Suitable Helper couples who put Ken and Barbie to shame, the prayerful powerbrokers who keep the minister and the church coffers on a tight leash — reminds me that I'm not the "right" kind of Christian.

How could I ever be one of God's girls when my deceased dad was a renegade Episcopal priest and college professor? The Rev. Dr. Karl Claudius Garrison Jr. might have hailed from the Bible Belt, but he sought salvation from a bottle of Southern Comfort.

Then again, take a good look at Jesus' crew. They were the unclean, the unchosen, the unloved — the very people discarded by the religious establishment. What a bunch of missional misfits. No way would they be allowed to play on most Christian teams.

Here's what I don't get: Jesus' life, death, and resurrection turned his followers' lives upside down. So if those disciples were willing to give up everything they had, including their lives, to follow Jesus, then why are many Christians, myself included, such misguided messes? In the words of Mike Yaconelli, the founder of *The Wittenburg Door* and my first editor, "What happened to the category-smashing, life-threatening, anti-institutional gospel that spread through the first century like wildfire and was considered (by those in power) *dangerous*?" What the J is going on?

As we've seen all too often, some Christians seek out the glare of the media spotlight as though this man-made electricity represents the true light of the world. In their mission to become the ringmasters of the Religious Ringling Brothers & Biblical Barnum Bailey Circus, they compete with their fellow clowns to headline "The Greatest Show on Heaven and Earth."

Ever wonder what Jesus thinks when Christians pretend to glorify his name while placing themselves in the center ring? Does he ever turn to his dad and go, "I died for this?"

Christians may claim to love this humble carpenter from Nazareth, but we don't act Christlike a lot of the time. Wading through biblical bunk, evangelical excesses, and undemocratic dogma searching for signs of Jesus reminds me of the eager desperation one finds in small children trying to find Waldo (or Wally, if you're based in the UK). It's tough, but eventually they spot Waldo's striped shirt and goofy glasses.

Likewise, once I look beyond the ungodly glitz and Jesus junk, I can spot ordinary radicals operating below the spiritual radar. They're so busy trying to figure out how to put the Beatitudes into practice that they don't bother to pimp out their products (Matthew 5–7). You won't find them issuing manifestos, proclamations, and declarations as pious proof they've created this magic elixir that will somehow "save" the Christian church. They remind me a bit of holy hobbits — for years I seldom saw them in action, but once I started training my eye to look out for these everyday saints, I kept noticing them everywhere I looked.

In January 2007, I began a series of business and personal travels, starting with my first trip to Israel. During these trips, I started observing what religion scholar Phyllis Tickle terms "the Great Emergence," a period of massive societal upheaval impacting technology, science, politics, religion, and the global culture at large.

With each step forward in my faith, I find myself trying to connect with the soil and souls of those who walked this way before me. Through their stories, we can see these threads of church history and tradition woven into the fabric of the future. Whenever I find myself wandering in the wilderness, it's usually because I went off in my own direction instead of continuing along this ancient pilgrim path.

During this research, I stumbled upon Phil Cousineau's book *The Art of Pilgrimage*, a slim volume that proved to be a valuable tool to help ground me in my journeys. Cousineau defines pilgrimage as "the art of movement, the poetry of motion, the music of personal experience of the sacred in those places where it has been known to shine forth. If we are not astounded by these possibilities, we can never plumb the depths of our souls or the soul of the world."

Anyone who knows me will testify that the thought of me engaged in quiet contemplation gives them the giggles. I resemble a chatterbox, not a contemplative. From a very early age, I learned to use humor as a defense mechanism that enabled me to survive as my nuclear family detonated. So naturally, I turn on the snark and fast-talk my way out of a prickly situation.

But something kept tugging at my heart, telling me I needed to go deeper, much deeper. After all, I am related to John Howland, John Alden, and Priscilla Mullins, who were three passengers aboard the *Mayflower*. Perhaps there's some presence of this ancestral pilgrim spirit embedded into my DNA.

Despite this tenuous historical pilgrim connection, I confess that I'm a newbie in this whole pilgrimage process. Hence I began a flurry of emails with the Rev. Kurt Neilson, author of *Urban Iona*. How could the insights he gleaned from his pilgrimage to Ireland and Scotland assist me in my conversion from traveler to spiritual seeker? He reminded me that I need to be open to see, taste, hear, feel, or smell whatever I come across and then let that transform me. Accept whatever happens and don't try to fight it. Not exactly words a control freak like me likes to hear. But the nudging in my gut kept telling me he was onto something, and that I should stop talking and listen for once.

After I quieted down, I had to admit to the painful truth that, while I interviewed people about their spiritual journeys all the time, I had forgotten the last time I really spoke to Jesus. Every time I tried to pray, I felt like this rabid dog trying to catch its ever-elusive tail. Every so often, my circular motions would land me into a labyrinth, where I could stop for a bit and catch my breath. But then it was right back on the holy hamster wheel once again.

But Kurt's gentle voice kept pushing me forward. "The journey is the goal. And the road is made by walking. Been said by many, in so many words, more or less."

Holy Land Happenings

JANUARY 2007

In my faith fantasy, my first trek to Jesus' stomping ground would be mystical and melodious, a singular spiritual sensation — imagine a musical version of Franco Zeffirelli's *Jesus of Nazareth* starring a 1970s-era hippie savior. But the U.S. State Department's security alerts set a sterner tone.

When I got the news that I could join a small contingent of evangelical writers on a press trip to Israel, I did my homework and secured some article assignments — all the while doubting that the promised trip would ever actually happen. Even as I checked in with El Al Airlines and boarded the plane, I thought I might get punk'd. Then it hit me midair — *Oh my God, I'm actually going to Israel!*

En route, I skimmed my complimentary copy of Fodor's *Israel* and soaked in *The Bible Experience*, an audio version of the New Testament. I listened to Cuba Gooding voicing the role of Jesus, but the real people showing me the money were the Israeli businessmen talking rather loudly behind me. After my laptop batteries and my fellow passengers ran out of juice, all was quiet, and I was able to get a few hours of sleep during this nine-hour flight.

We arrived at Ben Gurion International Airport at the crack of dawn. Shalom signs everywhere welcomed us to the Holy Land. I expected to see merchants selling Christendom crud, kosher kitsch, and Islamic trinkets, but instead I bumped into a sea of Orthodox frequent flyers and a smattering of largely Western European travelers. That and the Guns N' Moses display: baby-faced Israeli soldiers armed with automatic weapons everywhere I looked.

HOLY PLACE

NO DOGS, CIGARETTS,
GUNS & SHORT CLOTHING!

After a quick breakfast, our guide showed us around Tel Aviv and the neighboring town of Jaffa (Joppa), the town where Jonah boarded a boat while fleeing from God. Seeing the whale sculpture gave me a case of the Christian chuckles, a malady that I sensed irritated a few of my fellow travelers, who seemed to be taking a more serious approach.

After we swallowed the whale story, the day took on a more somber tone when we passed by the site where Prime Minister Yitzhak Rabin was assassinated on November 4, 1995, by right-wing Israeli radical Yigal Amir. Given the amount of press coverage this event received in New York City, somehow I thought his memorial would be overflowing with candles and professional mourners. But the rock that marked the spot where Rabin breathed his last was adorned with a simple wreath of flowers. I guess if they lit candles for everyone killed over the centuries by some crazed fanatic, then all of Israel would be ablaze.

The Sea of Galilee Circus

Yesterday we had a taste of the Old Testament, and today we were off to explore New Testament territory. As we tooled around the seaside town of Caesarea, I shook my head in disbelief. I expected something high and holy, seeing that this was the place where Paul was imprisoned for two years before setting sail for Rome (Acts 23–27). But Pilate's playpen looked like one of those overpriced luxury resorts marketed to those who possess more cash than common sense.

My feeling of nothingness was a foretaste of the spiritual letdowns that awaited me.

"This is it?!"

We're standing at Megiddo, the spot where — according to the predestination police — Armageddon's going to get you. I always thought the launch pad where the LaHaye & Jenkins Armageddon Action Team® takes off on the Heaven Bound Express™ would be a site of biblical proportions. Even Mount Everest would be a pebble by comparison. The Rapture Ready crew never mentioned that the final judgment for all of humanity will take place on a plot of land the size of a suburban mini-mall.

Repairs to the underground tunnels prevented us from seeing much of the underbelly of this hill that is set on top of the ruins of twenty-six different cities. Each time Israel was conquered, the victor razed the land and built new structures that spoke to their particular sociopolitical and religious sensibilities.

But we did get to walk around a stone shack built for Christian worship services and tour the ruins of the Megiddo stables. When our guide identified a rough-hewn stone slab as a manger, I stood there stunned. This isn't the cute wooden rock-a-bye baby crib portrayed in countless Christmas pageants and Hollywood depictions of the baby Jesus, but a grimy, ratty relic. In this desert climate, wood was such a precious commodity that building a feeding trough out of this resource would indeed be casting pearls before swine.

This manger brought to mind the mangled nativity set my family kept on our mantelpiece. Every so often, our overeager beagles thought a wise man would make for a tasty treat — we never bought into the whole "Do not give dogs what is sacred" thing (Matthew 7:6). (Fortunately, our clueless canines never ate the baby Jesus. Communion issues aside, chomping down on this diminutive doll would have sent them to the vet, or worse.)

Frankly, Megiddo reminded me of the straggly renditions of faith I find scattered throughout a Flannery O'Connor short story. Like one of her characters returning from the dead, would the winds of radical redemption breathe life into these ruins (Ezekiel 37:1–14)? 'Cause at that point, I was feeling more heretical than holy.

On to Nazareth — the badlands where the baby king became a carpenter kid. I wasn't keen to do a point-by-point comparison of Isaiah 53 to the New Testament birth narratives; but when I walked down those narrow stone streets, I understood why people scoffed when they heard that the Messiah hailed from Nazareth (John 1:46). There wasn't much beauty or majesty emanating from this isolated backwater town that is currently inhabited by a largely Arab population.

No trip to Christ's crib would be complete without a visit to Nazareth Village, a community theater–styled production depicting life as it "might have been" when Jesus walked on this earth. All throughout their "performance," I just couldn't bring myself to "interact" with the "actors." (And yes, I am using that term loosely.) I refrained from any Lamb of God lampoons, camel cracks, or sheep 'n' goat gaffes at the risk of offending our hosts, but this was getting way too Disneyfied for my tastes. I'm just not seeing anyone in Nazareth who even remotely resembles the Westernized depictions of Jesus as this wimpy WASP who can barely lift a hammer, let alone assist his father in the carpentry biz. (The Bible never says if Jesus actually worked as a carpenter, though I suspect he helped his father out when he wasn't doing moves like running off to the temple [Luke 2:39–52].) So what gives with selling blue-eyed baby Jesus dolls?

Nazareth Village Products

This town's angelic afterglow made me queasy. I just don't buy the spiritual shtick where the archangel Gabriel floats down to a harp sound track.

"Pardon me. Would you care to join me for a cup of tea?"

"Why, yes."

"I take it you like the birth of your son, our Lord and Savior, served sweet with milk and honey?"

No way. Instead, here's how the gospel of Luke recounts this interaction:

> The angel went to [Mary] and said, "Greetings, you who are highly favored! The Lord is with you." Mary was greatly troubled at his words and wondered what kind of greeting this might be. But the angel said to her, "Do not be afraid, Mary, you have found favor with God."
>
> LUKE 1:28–30

Why would an angel need to offer words of comfort unless poor Mary was shaking in her sandals? Frankly, I don't blame her. If Gabriel came knocking on my door, I'm pretty sure I'd run for the hills (or worse). I get the strong sense Tony Kushner got it right in *Angels in America* when he depicted angels as major heinie kickers — and props to Frank Peretti for his imagination, if not his literary virtuosity. Survey the medieval masterpieces depicting that moment when God's mighty messengers descend upon us mere mortals, and it's pretty clear what's missing. Where's the puddle on the floor?

As our tour guide pointed out certain "historical" sites scattered throughout Nazareth, I found myself getting increasingly frustrated. Yes, I know archaeology matters. But I'm also aware that during the Crusades, a market developed to peddle a place as a "sacred" spot — a practice that obviously continues to this day. For example, multiple churches in Nazareth claim to be the place where Gabriel appeared to Mary. But do we really have to pinpoint the exact location of the annunciation? Can we? Doesn't it matter more that God became man and dwelt among us? That's the event I want to explore further.

While I don't seek to diminish the reams of biblical scholarship, I am concerned that if I scrutinize every theological tree, I'll miss the faith forest. After all, do we prove we are Christians by unearthing historical artifacts or by following the Great Commandment (Matthew 22:36–40; Mark 12:28–31)? If our faith is a living entity, why do we get fixated on the past? Too often, we get so busy looking for ancient stones that we're blind to the current realities in front of us.

Sea of Galilee, Take Two

Olive presses and cisterns and fallen foundations, oh my! After a certain point, sacred sites become a biblical blur. Every so often, we'd visit a spot like Capernaum, where enough archaeological evidence had been unearthed that one could sort of picture St. Peter relaxing at home. But for the most part, all that's left is rubble. Not only was I not finding Jesus, but my satirical self was starting to get the better of me. Given the more studious nature of my traveling companions, I kept my cracks to myself. I doubt they'd be amused by the BBQ jokes I muttered under my breath while we toured Kursi (Matthew 8:28–34), the traditional location where Jesus drove the demons out of two men and into a herd of pigs.

I felt a bit guilty for thinking silly thoughts while walking on supposedly holy ground, but how else could a satirist respond when coming across, say, a fish fountain at Tabgha that commemorates the miracle of the multiplication of the loaves and fishes? No way did Jesus feed the crowd brightly colored goldfish (Matthew 14:13–21; Mark 6:31–44; Luke 9:10–17; John 6:5–13). Seems to me a feeding program would be a more appropriate living metaphor than a gift shop, but by now it's clear that these commemorative churches gear themselves to the tourist trade instead of the wandering stranger in need.

At first I envisioned building a spitting station in Bethsaida to commemorate Jesus' healing of the blind man by spitting on his eyes (Mark 8:22–26; John 9:1–12), but then my eye spotted two gigantic D-rings. Our guide was more interested in describing the remains of the winegrower's house than illuminating why these D-rings were left behind in the aftermath of the Six-Day War (also called the 1967 War), but I couldn't take my mind off this pile of debris sitting there in plain view. Scholars have yet to unlock the scholarly secret behind Jesus' healing miracles. However, these D-rings serve as a visible reminder that we're still blind to the possibilities for peace.

But just because a person is blind, does that mean they really want to undergo the process of regaining their sight? Taking the miracle at Bethsaida at its most literal level, how many of us would sit still while some stranger covered our faces with mud and then spit on us? What's more, what happened when the man finally got his sight back and walked around the town a bit? Did he like what he saw? What if he was so accustomed to imagining the world as he thought it should look that he couldn't deal with reality staring him in the face? Let's face it, many of us see life through a faith fog; we're not so interested in having our vision corrected.

D-rings on display

On a side note, the man now lacked the visible infirmity that enabled him to eke out a living through begging. Once reality set in, did this man realize that without any marketable skills whatsoever he would find it very difficult to support himself? If I were in his shoes, I'm not so certain I'd possess this blind faith that God would provide for all my needs. Can I really not worry about my life and put all my trust in God? I'd like to say yes (Matthew 6:25–27), but some days I seem to have OD'd on doubt.

Despite the presence of D-rings, at least we could walk around Bethsaida. As much as I wanted to romp around the Golan Heights, I couldn't. Too many land mines and unbiblical bunkers remain hidden in those holy hills. After our guide brought up this jarring fact, he returned to his task of pointing out the locations of Mount Tabor, Tiberius, and other well-known sites. But I kept thinking about how this holy ground continues to be desecrated. Surely this wasn't Jesus' intended outcome when the Prince of Peace came to Galilee.

When I saw the Sea of Galilee from atop the Golan Heights, I froze. Stunned. Silenced.

I've fly-fished on bigger lakes than this. Somehow I expected the Son of God to have bigger faith footprints. Given that the entire circumference of this lake is approximately thirty-three miles, Jesus could have easily walked from town to town.

My stomach rumbled. I'd like to say I was getting some divine revelation that would give me some insights into this connection between the touristy and the theological; but more likely I was just jonesing for a bit of St. Peter's fish.

Sea of Galilee — Gone Fishing

Even in the Holy Land, it's possible to wake up at an ungodly hour. Since I was up, I figured I might as well watch the sunrise over the Sea of Galilee. I traipsed on down to the lake and found a spot away from the fishermen that enabled me to reflect without getting hooked.

Slowly, the sky turned from a misty dark-bluish hue to a bright-purplish haze. Then the firmament seemed to settle down. That was a nice moment. At least I got a few shots of men casting their nets and the Galilee Experience Museum that I could add to my selection of funny Bible pics.

But just as I started to turn away, rays of light pierced though the skyline. I couldn't move. If I wasn't such a cynic, I'd swear God zapped me to ensure I didn't miss the rising of his Son's sun. Within a matter of minutes, the entire sky burst into this bright orange fire. I've lost track of the number of sun dances I've seen in my years of fly-fishing, hiking, kayaking, and sailing. But I can't remember the sun ever God-smacking me like this. Flecks of gold glitter winked at me, daring me to join in their water dance.

At that moment I knew for certain that God is no delusion. No, I can't prove it empirically, but I know it in my bones. I cover Christian carnage for a living. Lord knows, I'm not about to defend the follies of the faith. But maybe the end of frozen faith could be the beginning of trying to follow the path of Jesus, even if this means traversing the land mines in the Golan Heights. We just have to open up our heart to the Son.

Like Peter, James, and John, I wanted to stay and bask like a bodhisattva in God's light (Mark 9:5–6). But I realized I needed to grab breakfast because pretty soon it would be time to go, go, go.

If the Sea of Galilee was smaller than I expected, then the mighty Jordan River was a miniature creek. That water is barely waist high — heck, in places it barely washes over one's ankles. These baby bodies of holy water reminded me of just how small and human Jesus really was. From these simple beginnings, Christianity was born.

At Yardinet, one could purchase a baptismal robe with an accompanying certificate and receive a proper dunking, provided one had the right amount of cha-ching. As a major connoisseur of Christian crud, I have to say that the Holy Land–branded products rivaled anything I've seen in the United States. (Then again, I haven't been to Trinity Broadcast Network's (TBN) Holy Land Experience theme park in Orlando, Florida. So I haven't had the opportunity to shop at the Old Scroll or Shofar shops or have an unkosher hot dog at Simeon's Corner. However, during the "Adventures in Travel" Expo, TBN had a booth where I came face-to-face with Fabio Jesus, Caiaphas, and a Centurion.) The Christian cheese wafted through this Jesus joint — think ungodly Gouda meets sacrilegious Swiss. Can you really bottle holy water and take it home? Tempted as I was to test this theological theory, I didn't give in — because, fortunately, we had to leave before I surrendered my shekels.

Our driver sped through the Jordan Valley on the way to Masada, passing by the refugee camps and other locations in the

West Bank considered off-limits to the tourist trade. We wouldn't go to the Cave of the Patriarchs in Hebron or to Jericho, where, according to Joshua, the walls came tumbling down (Joshua 6:20). But I can't contemplate archaeological disputes right now. I'm chilled to the core at the sight of children of God confined by man-made walls of war.

Jesus wept.
John 11:35

These are the voiceless whom Christ came to save, yet we're going so fast I can't even take a picture of these shacks to try to tell their story. However, we did stop to photograph three young shepherds tending their sheep. I wanted to talk to these teens, but our guide discouraged any interaction.

We were given a typical afternoon tour of the West Bank — Masada, Qumran, the Dead Sea — followed by dinner at a West Bank restaurant. Such spiritual safaris provide safe and sanitized expeditions to this volatile region, where one can see the preapproved holy sites without getting all devotionally dirty. God forbid that comfy Christians should actually interact with their impure Palestinian brothers and sisters.

My eyes were drawn to the heightened security that greeted us at every turn. I shudder to think how those traveling without an approved tour guide might get treated.

"See how we all get along."

Despite this repeated Barneyesque mantra, I got the clear sense this was not much more than a well-rehearsed beauty pageant.

Jerusalem 'n' Jesus

Our harried schedule didn't allow me any free time to watch the news. So I was shocked to learn that United States Secretary of State Condoleezza Rice was there. In Jerusalem. Bunkered in the David Citadel Hotel. Did I mention we were staying at the David Citadel Hotel? Lovely. I had adjusted to the sight of baby-faced youth decked out in military garb and toting assault rifles, but it really got my goat that I had to pass by a steady stream of soldiers just so I could get to my hotel room.

Every morning, Rice's bevy of black SUVs careened toward Ramallah, the Gaza Strip, and other hot spots deemed out-of-bounds to most journalists. (Since we're on the subject of "off-limits," I learned that since 2000, the Dome of the Rock remains closed to the tourist trade. The reason why depends on who you ask.)

I got to thinking. What if Condi and I were to have a *Freaky Friday* moment and actually switched places? Now, I have no interest in being a war correspondent or working for any government entity. Something tells me the Bush administration lacked a funny bone. Long term, this arrangement would never ever work.

Still, what would it look like for me to bear the burden of Bush while she satirized the religious landscape in search of signs of the risen Christ? Could I handle the tense negotiations she dealt with in Ramallah without cracking up? Do the soldiers patrolling the hotel give her the willies as well? Who does

"AH, MY PALESTINIAN FRIEND, ONCE THE ROMANS ARE GONE, OUR PEOPLES WILL LIVE FOREVER IN PEACE AND HARMONY!"

she feel is being left behind in the peace process? Tempted though I might be to saunter up to her hotel suite for a chat, the soldiers staring at me in the lobby tell me to just walk on by.

> *Despite the reference in the psalms to "the peace of Jerusalem," the Holy City has probably seen more rapine and pillage, more regularly, than any comparable patch of ground on the planet.... Its soil is drenched in blood spilt in the name of religion; its mental hospitals are full of whole hagiarchies of lunatics claiming to be David, Isaiah, Jesus, St. Paul or Mohammed.*
>
> **William Dalrymple,** *From the Holy Mountain*

Over the next three days, we hit the theological tourist trifecta, running through centuries of holy history lickety-split. We took a religious roller-coaster ride on the Via Dolorosa, where we whooshed through the Stations of the Cross so quickly it was as if Lent lasted only forty minutes, not forty days. Here's the spot where the virgin Mary was born ... the place where John the Baptist's head was buried ... the alleged stone where the Roman soldiers cast lots for Jesus' robe ... the crack where Judas (or, as storyteller Rob Lacey liked to call him, the "sell-out specialist") stubbed his big toe (what a whiney baby). After a while you could almost hear the stones vying for spiritual supremacy, with each pebble claiming to be the rock on which St. Peter built the church (Matthew 16:18).

Everywhere I turned, I stumbled upon some believer paying and praying for their piece of the pilgrimage. I didn't spot any donkeys for hire, though we were able to survey the Mount of Olives courtesy of the requisite camel ride. Committed Christians can reenact Jesus' Good Friday experience by renting life-size wooden crosses. They even come with wheels, so one can retrace Christ's walk to

Calvary while avoiding that Simon of Cyrene backache (Matthew 27:32; Mark 15:21; Luke 23:26).

I knew Jerusalem was divided into four quarters — Muslim, Christian, Armenian, and Jewish — but I had no clue just how much these groups rubbed up against each other. Merchants inhabited every available space in the markets, hawking everything from "Don't Worry, Be Jewish" T-shirts to stuffed camels donned in faux Israeli army gear. I lost track of the number of times I had to mumble a quick prayer to keep myself from turning over these tables. Living in New York City, I've developed a very high tolerance for ornery crowds, but I didn't see how anyone could live in this place and keep their sanity and spirituality intact.

Tomb Trash-Talkin'

Both the Catholic/Orthodox Church of the Holy Sepulchre and the Protestant Garden Tomb claim to be the spot where Jesus suffered death, was buried, and rose again. We were ushered into the Church of the Holy Sepulchre after standing in line, lemminglike.

The church, lit only by candles and the light shining in from the stained glass windows, felt more like the movie set for the latest teen vampire flick than the holiest of holies. As soon as we stepped inside this sacred space, we got shoved into a line facing an ornate altar. There it was — the "very rock" where Jesus was crucified. I knelt and tried to say a quick prayer, but someone elbowed me in the back. Time's up. Next.

On our way to explore a few tombs and other underground delights, we passed another view of the "very rock" ensconced in glass that was constantly cleaned and polished by workers.

Then we waited in yet another line. This highly decorated kiosk containing the tomb where Jesus was laid looked more like an ornate dollhouse for a spoiled princess than the resting place for the Savior. A stern white-bearded cleric monitored every move of those who dared to enter this monument. Undaunted by his glare, we entered the tomb only to be told to exit almost immediately.

> *One hopes for peace, but the ear is assailed by a cacophony of warring chants. One desires holiness, only to encounter a jealous possessiveness: the six groups of occupants — Latin Catholics, Greek Orthodox, Armenian Orthodox, Syrians, Copts, Ethiopians — watch one another suspiciously for any infringement of rights. The fragility of humanity is nowhere more apparent than here; it epitomizes the human condition.*
>
> **Jerome Murphy-O'Connor,** *The Holy Land*

Jump down, turn around, touch the ground where they laid the Lord. Here we go — religious "Ring around the Rosie." No matter where I went, I kept banging into yet another group laying claim to their specific sacred space.

These monks in black, all of whom looked like they had OD'd on prunes, didn't take too kindly to Christian chicks. How dare I interfere with their priestly posturing? One look into their eagle eyes and I could see how they had become consumed with being right and rigid.

Our pit stop at the Wailing Wall and our quick trek through the Mea Shearim section of Jerusalem also reminded me that as a woman, I'm not exactly welcome in some religious circles.

How did the site where Jesus Christ gave his life for all devolve into such a Christian circus? Don't these religious relics realize that their gilded crucifixes symbolize that through Christ I am deemed equal in his eyes? In their faith frenzy, somehow they forgot how Jesus redeemed those who were created human by God (see Genesis 1–2) but were now being treated in the first century CE as chattel.

Yes, slavery remains a sordid stain on our collective humanity. Still, the vast majority of us cannot comprehend growing up in a culture where women get accorded the same status as the family donkey. How threatening it must have been for a patriarchal culture to be faced with such potential financial losses should their female property be set free! Yet today, these visible signs of Jesus' death and resurrection remain under lock and key, guarded by these monks in black.

On our way out, I almost tripped over a few women who were ceremoniously wiping down the alleged table where Jesus' body was laid. Why are they relegated to the spiritual sidelines yet again? I say a prayer for the day when we can get all biblical and let these contemporary women take their rightful place as guardians of his cross and the empty tomb.

After all, who was the very first person to witness the risen Christ (Matthew 28:1–10; Mark 16:1–8; Luke 24:1–10; John 20:1–18)? I'm going to go medieval on anyone who calls Mary Magdalene a prostitute. To those who claim the resurrection is a faithless fairy tale, consider this. If the disciples cooked up this Christian concoction, they wouldn't have their Messiah make his first appearance as the risen Lord before a lowly woman. Such a move would mark them as delusional at best. Even the disciples thought these women were spouting nonsense, thus demonstrating the lack of respect accorded to women in first-century Judea (Luke 24:11).

History seems to be written by the winners; therefore, church historians tend to focus on the actions of the male disciples. This revisionist history fails to mention that after the eleven remaining disciples hightailed it out of there, a few women stood vigil at the foot of the cross. Later they assisted in the burial of the only man who truly embraced them as equals in the kingdom of God (Matthew 27:55–61; Mark 15:40–48; Luke 23:49–56).

But do a bit of digging and one can unearth women like Anna, the only person designated in the New Testament as a prophet (Luke 2:36–38). She was the first person to recognize the Messiah without being prompted. (Yes, according to the nativity story [Luke 2:1–12], the shepherds and Wise Men were the first to see the baby Jesus, but they were guided by an angel, whereas Anna had this revelation all on her own.) Following Jesus' unclean and very public interactions with a Samaritan woman at a public well, he made the front page of *The Pharisee Post* (John 4:4–26). He extended mercy to a woman about to be stoned for adultery (John 8:1–11). Over his disciples' protests, he welcomed a female sinner who crashed a dinner party so she could anoint his feet with oil (Luke 7:36–50). As much as Jesus enjoyed Martha's cooking, he encouraged Mary to join the all-boys theological discussion instead of washing dishes (Luke 10:38–42).

After Jesus learned that his mother and brothers were looking for him, Jesus looked at those sitting in the circle around him and responded, "Here are my mother and my brothers!" (Mark 3:34). According to the Jewish customs of the time, Jesus would not have said "mother and brothers" had there not been female disciples gathered around him. So if one wants to really be like Jesus, then propping up an all-male ministerial brigade sounds downright unbiblical.

Now that I've worked myself up into a full-blown rant, I suddenly realize I've fallen into that all-too-common mistake of thrusting my Western sensibilities on a group of Orthodox women I've never even met. Once again, my ways are not their ways.

Unfortunately, we didn't have the time for me to turn around so I could explore their story further. Why were they drawn to that table? What does it mean for them to caress and pray over that relic? But even if I could go back, thrusting a mic in someone's face while she's immersed in performing a ritual sounds a bit too FOX-newsworthy for my style.

Onward to the Protestant Garden Tomb. This site's main claim to fame appeared to be that this rocky outcrop outside the city walls constitutes Calvary. There *is* a quasi-depiction of a skull that could be a reference to Golgotha ("the place of the skull," Matthew 27:33), in the same way one can find Mother Teresa in a sticky bun, the Virgin Mary in a water stain, or the Lamb of God in a cloud formation.

Did the Garden Tomb hold the body of Jesus? Doubtful, given that this site was discovered in 1867 and people were visiting the site where the Church of the Holy Sepulchre stands even before Constantine built a church on that spot in 326 BCE. Still, I felt much more connected to the Garden Tomb. This place felt serene, secure, safe.

> *We have this uncanny ability to find God in the oddest of places. Everywhere, it seems, but in the faces of all those people we don't like —*
> *our enemies.*
> **Karen Spears Zacharias,**
> *Where's Your Jesus Now?*

But I can't have a pastoral passion because that's not how the crucifixion went down. Even if you discount chunks of Mel Gibson's *The Passion of the Christ* bloodbath, we're talking a dark night of the soul where even St. John of the Cross reaches for the Prozac. Fragile. Forgotten. Forsaken. I'd better stop with the Fs right about now. We want to skip over this seemingly blasphemous bit where Jesus descended into hell before rising again and ushering in a new creation because it gets in the way of our candy-coated beatitudes. We peeps want our Easter served on a silver platter — less Mel and more marshmallows.

> *I* *believe it was the tiger-philosopher Hobbes who described human life as "solitary, poor, nasty, brutish, and short." Religion allows us to ignore all that by praying.*
> **Stephen Colbert,** *I Am America (And So Can You!)*

As I departed the Garden Tomb — God forgive me for thinking sacrilegious thoughts — I started humming that Monty Python mantra "Always Look on the Bright Side of Life." God bless Brian.

Bethlehem Beatitudes

Bethlehem wasn't on our "official" itinerary, and our Israeli guide could not escort us in Palestine because Israeli citizens cannot enter Palestine and vice versa. Still, I felt I couldn't leave Israel without at least a peek inside this holy city. Given we had a half day of "free travel," I decided to go there on my own. I made plans with the Rev. Dr. Mitri Raheb, senior pastor of the Evangelical Lutheran Christmas Church, to attend their Sunday morning church service. He seemed to have his faith fingers in a number of pastoral pies, as he also served as general director for the International Center of Bethlehem and president of Diyar Consortium. Good man to know.

After I joined two other journalists for a quick cab ride to the Little Town of Bethlehem (no donkey rides, dang it), we came face-to-face with the infamous twenty-five-foot barricade constructed to separate Bethlehem from Israel. I was expecting security snafus, but the lone guard at the entrance ushered us through very quickly. Then we went our own ways, me in a cab to Manger Square.

Most of the stores were closed until after the morning church services. But I doubted they'd do much business that day anyway. Except for a few soldiers guarding the Church of the Nativity, I felt like I almost had the square to myself. The streets were quiet — too quiet.

The Twelve Days of Christmas had come and gone, but merchants still kept Christmas decorations in their windows. Santa graced the lobby of the Bethlehem Peace Center as though somehow

his elfin magic would help alleviate the massive drop in tourism that has decimated this tiny town.

An armed guard pointed me toward the Door of Humility, the only way in to this sixth-century church. During the Ottoman era, this small, rectangle-shaped stone door was modified to keep looters from ransacking the place. Forget about trying to make a regal entrance — there's nothing glamorous at all about crouching down caveman style.

Rays of light from a few windows and rows of votive candles partially illuminated the sparely decorated cavernous interior. A small crowd watched the Orthodox service already in progress at the high altar. Unfortunately, the actual cave that marks the traditional site of Christ's birth was closed until after the Sunday morning services. I hoped the calming presence I felt meant that the Roman Catholic and Armenian and Greek Orthodox clerics who share custody of this space had worked out their differences, unlike their counterparts over at the Church of the Holy Sepulchre in Jerusalem.

When I stopped off at the International Center of Bethlehem and saw the sculptures created out of bits from bomb blasts on display, I became too stunned to even take a photograph. Seeing is indeed believing. Why have we as American Christians allowed for the birthplace of our Lord and Savior to become bombed-out Bethlehem? I know Jesus was born in a barn, but do our sermons have to smell like one as well? I don't know about you, but I think it's high time we started mucking out the stables.

I began walking toward the Evangelical Lutheran Christmas Church, a white oasis that stood smack-dab in the middle of Market Square. I felt more than a bit out of place being the only tourist in a sea of hijabs, burkas, and skullcaps. Older women and those with disabilities sat on the stone streets, surrounded by baskets of dust-covered dates and other wares, while the more agile merchants shoved their offerings in my face, hoping I'd make a purchase. I sensed the desperation in their eyes and wished I could do something. But I realized I couldn't buy from one merchant without creating a mini-stampede of sorts.

I chatted briefly with Mitri Raheb before the service began, and I wished we had more time to connect. Although the service was mostly in Arabic, I found I could follow along with the liturgical flow of the service. Mitri's quiet presence as he led the congregation in worship filled me with such a sense of calm that I began to get an inkling of this peace that passes all understanding.

After the service, we joined the small congregation and a visiting Lutheran tour group for a bit of coffee. My itinerary said go, but my heart wanted to stay and immerse myself in the life of this community.

We crossed into Bethlehem with ease, so naturally we expected a similar transition back to Jerusalem. Instead, we were greeted by the sights and sounds of Palestinians trying, often in vain, to cross the border. Their requests seemed so routine to me. They needed to see a doctor, visit their family, earn a few shekels, and carry out other trips that I take for granted. I wish I could have photographed the site of this cattle call, but the guards' gazes indicated I shouldn't even think about attempting such a misguided move.

Such is the daily life for a Palestinian, whose everyday existence is dictated by the security measures enacted throughout the West Bank, East Jerusalem, and Palestine. As ongoing acts of terrorism indicate, criminals can always find ways to circumvent the system. So instead of protecting Israeli citizens from terrorists, these actions further divide this war-torn region. People have lost their livelihood because they could not get to their places of employment. Farmers whose land is on one side of the wall and home is on the other can no longer tend to their crops. When someone needs advanced medical care, they cannot leave Palestine to seek out a specialist. And the stories go on ad infinitum.

Reaching the gate didn't mean I was out of the woods yet. Every time I tried to pass through the metal detector, it beeped. Loudly. Emptied purse. Beep. Took off all jewelry. Beep. Now shoes. Beep. Removed all items from pockets. Beep. Beep. Dang, it's the buckles on my pants. These same travel trousers passed El Al's intense security system, so I thought they were A-OK. Obviously, I was mistaken. Beep. Beep. Beep. Oh my God. Beep. Beep. Beep.

> *Why don't you treat me like a human? I am a human after all.*
> **Jonny Baker and Jon Birch,** "Human"

Do I have to take my pants off in Palestine? Fortunately, they finally let me go. I guess seeing me in my unmentionables would have shamed them too much. (Not to worry. I still had on clean underwear, though I'm not sure how long I could have kept myself safe and sanitary under these conditions.)

On the cab ride back to Jerusalem, I looked out the window and fumed. Why was I as a Westernized Christian allowed to travel around most of the world as I pleased, while all those living in Bethlehem could not even leave their borders? Maybe, just maybe, we're asking the wrong questions. Yes, I know that what America does militarily matters. Obviously, the lives of U.S. citizens and those some political and religious leaders deemed "our enemies" changed dramatically post-9/11. But I just met people who have never known peace, though they live where the Prince of Peace was born.

While Jesus extended agape to all, if he came back to earth, I suspect he would demand an end to such a mockery of his mission. Maybe I've just been reading the wrong non-red-letter versions of the Bible, but the Jesus of Nazareth I follow showed solidarity with the poor and oppressed. So when will those who claim Jesus Christ as their personal Lord and Savior follow the lead of Religious Right icon Ronald Reagan and start chanting, "Tear Down This Wall"?

Getting God-Smacked

Somehow in the midst of all this Christian craziness, I managed to catch fleeting glimpses of God's redeeming love. I continued my ritual of waking up around sunrise so I could savor the sacred silence.

Peering out toward East Jerusalem, I could see the sun breaking through. I'd like to believe there's hope on the horizon. But the purplish haze and orange hues that greeted me couldn't hide the bulldozed and bullet-riddled settlements I spotted off in the distance. Nor could the sun conceal the excavation of the City of David, a venture that's either Bible blessed or yet another means of displacing Palestinian settlers. Once again, each side has its own story as to the history behind this walled-off war zone.

During my last day in Israel, while the sun rose over Jerusalem, a rooster crowed in the background. At that moment, I had a flashback to Peter's rooster revelation (Luke 22:34). The presence of God's saving grace throughout history hit me in a visceral way, as though some theological two-by-four had whopped me upside the head. Before I had a chance to reflect on all those times when I've petered out, a pack of stray dogs ran toward me. They chased me up a small tree, Zacchaeus style (Luke 19:4). I tried to stay as still as possible, praying the dogs would stop baring their teeth at me. Finally they ran off in pursuit of some other unsuspecting prey.

So much for magical moments.

I started to rush back to my hotel, grateful I escaped a trip to the hospital for a dog bite or worse, but then I remembered our guide telling us that families hold bar mitzvahs at the Wailing Wall on Mondays. So I decided to walk over and check it out.

As I stood off to the side of the men's section of the wall, I began to lose myself in the rhythm of this pre–bar mitzvah setup ritual. The rabbi, male family members, and caterers all seemed to play their part. When we toured the Wailing Wall the day before, my brief trip to Bethlehem occupied my thoughts, and I felt disengaged from the women rushing to touch the wall. Today I still hung back, but I felt a bit more connected.

We spent our last day in Jerusalem museum hopping. The Shrine of the Book, which houses a collection of the Dead Sea Scrolls, stood before us like a giant white Hershey's Kiss. Despite this modernist structure, the dim interior lighting bathed these parchment documents with an ancient, golden glow.

Compare that reverence to the chaos I experienced upon

entering Yad Vashem: Holocaust Martyrs' and Heroes' Remembrance Authority. Our guide took us so fast through the museum that I barely had time to absorb the horrors that were unfolding before my eyes. Her nonstop narration, coupled with the throngs of visitors snapping photos and chatting, created a cacophony that rendered me unable to focus on the abominations that were on display before me.

Once she completed her whirlwind tour, our guide escorted us into an underground cavern that housed the Children's Memorial. She finally stopped talking and gave us a few moments of silence. Since no other tourists were visiting this spot, we had the room all to ourselves to sit and reflect. In the background, a recorded voice recited a haunting litany. Hearing the names, ages, and countries of origin brought these souls to life. They were no longer 1.5 million nameless faces but unique individuals, each with their own story. I'm not the type who likes to cry in public. So I put on my sunglasses so the others wouldn't see my eyes tearing up.

After a very quiet car ride back to the Old City, our guide took us to an uber-Orthodox fast-food place where I ordered my last shawarma. Fortunately, no one saw the bit of hummus and tahini that leaked out of my oversized sandwich and down my shirt. I was feeling pretty messy in more ways than one. I just couldn't turn off that litany of all those children who died so needlessly.

Now I see why Jesus wept over Jerusalem (Luke 19:41). We still weep today. I suspect we'll weep tomorrow. Yet life goes on.

When I went to church the following Sunday, the congregation sang "Jesus Came to the River Jordan" while I hummed along. (Trust me, it's better that way.) I envisioned myself skipping stones across this small creek. The focus of the gospel lesson and sub-sequent sermon was Jesus' commentary about how the scripture is fulfilled today (Luke 4:21). I know this sounds Kansas corny, but I could feel chills going down my spine. It was one of those rare instances when I connected with the Bible in a visceral way. This doubting Thomas actually touched the land that's home to the three Abrahamic faiths. Despite all the spiritual silliness that abounds throughout the Holy Land, this sacred soil smiles. Dirty ... dusty ... delivered. For in this grit and grime, God becomes real and revealed.

Cutting the Christian Cheese

JUNE 2007

> *When I peruse the titles in a Christian bookstore, I feel like I am the only klutz in the kingdom of God, a spiritual nincompoop lost in a shipful of brilliant biblical thinkers, an ungodly midget in a world of spiritual giants.*
>
> **Mike Yaconelli,** *Messy Spirituality*

I'm not a professional Christian conferencegoer. Religious satirists tend to be viewed askance, as though we entered the sacred sanctuary eating a cheese, bean, and broccoli burrito. God forbid we might cause a stink.

But after I signed the contract for my first book, *Red and Blue God, Black and Blue Church,* in 2005, my new editor informed me she was coming to New York City to attend Book Expo America (BEA). She suggested we meet, so I applied for a press pass and decided to give it a go.

Much to my surprise, religious publishers confessed to me in hushed tones, "I *love The Wittenburg Door.*" Who knew these guardians of Americana Christianity™ had a funny bone and, in fact, took a secret pleasure out of having their stuff satirized? We seemed to be the evangelicals' dirty little secret, the rag that's read under the covers of darkness at Wheaton College.

By the end of BEA, I came out of the closet as a religious satirist. And it was good. I left the Expo loaded to the gills with business cards, book galleys, and, of course, spiritual swag (stuff *we all* get) — the professional name given to promotional items ranging from hard candy wrapped in Scripture verses to furry faith critters. I was hooked.

By the time Book Expo America 2007 arrived, I was a seasoned vet, having successfully completed two Expos without losing my sanity or my spirituality. For the uninitiated, BEA started as an annual convention for largely secular booksellers and has since

morphed into a monster marathon featuring seminar series, schmooze fests, and, of course, sales. Literary lions, baby bestsellers, and the latest kiddie creations sit perched in the autographed section, greeting the throngs of literati wannabes. Publishing princesses don their best books in preparation for the bestseller ball. But like Cinderella's carriage, much of this product will turn into pumpkins.

Book Expos are no easy task for any author, for it is here that one sees exactly how one's book journeys from page to stage. Like watching sausage get made, seeing the inner workings of the book factory makes it kind of tricky to maintain one's passion or palate.

The more savvy publicists and publishers know how to walk that fine line between the promoting and pimping. They're the ones I go to for the good Godstuff. The rest provide me with more than ample *Door* fodder. Take, for example, the two lapsed-Catholics-turned-"humor"-writers who tried to market their anti-Catholic joke book by giving away "Baby Jesus stigmata cookies," a gag chock-full of theological, historical, and biblical inaccuracies. No wonder their crud tasted lousy.

As expected, the large publishers dominated the main stage of this three-ring circus, hawking their wares and using giveaways to push their product. Plastic Jesus figures give a tacit bobblehead approval to this madness.

A side of me wants to storm the exhibition halls and throw a temple tantrum. But I'd better leave the table-turning-over to Jesus. I do have to wonder how he'd feel if he saw himself branded like he was the newest shiny theological toy — Sing-along Savior, Jokester Jesus, Lock 'n' Load Lord, Contextual Christ, Postmodern Pal, or Money Messiah. Unlike some, I don't presume to know the inner workings of our Savior's soul, though I seriously doubt these depictions were on his mind when he contemplated the cross in Gethsemane.

Forget about trying to find any signs of the risen Christ. Something tells me Jesus of Nazareth doesn't exactly like "doing lunch" with his classier counterpart Commercial Christ®. Despite the business books proclaiming Jesus as the perfect model for today's corporate CEO, he doesn't own the proper Armani suit or even a decent pair of shoes. For sure, he'd get shown the door for blowing his stack at the suits one time too many and probably end up in jail for giving away all the company's assets.

Even though Jesus wasn't anywhere to be found at BEA, the anti-God gurus were there in full force. In a touch of irony, bestselling New Atheist icon Christopher Hitchens spoke during the same time slot when the booksellers brought out the booze. As much as this Whiskeypalian enjoys reenacting the miracle at the wedding at Cana (John 2:1–11), my professional obligations won out. I sat through Hitchens's heretical hooey, which, in true Shakespearean style, was full of sound and fury, signifying nothing. (Like the porter in *Macbeth*, this man doth drink and then protest too much about his manhood.) Why couldn't they have invited comedian Lewis Black instead? I like my atheists cool, not crude.

Watching Hitchens drenched in scotch, soaking up the atheist accolades as though he was the anointed Antichrist, got me thinking about those times when I've seen the fawning faithful behave likewise. How do those of us with a message get the dialogue started without "going on tour" accompanied by faithonistas and godly giggle groupies who can out-sashay Salome (Matthew 14:1 – 10; Mark 6:17 – 29)? Do we want to worship the Jonas Brothers or Jesus?

On his blog, author Kester Brewin asked a number of writers to respond to his question: "What are the 'grand challenges' for theology for the 21st century?" I answered: "The challenge is finding ways to communicate theological change without becoming yet another crass Christian marketing machine." Rob VanAlkemade, director of the documentary *What Would Jesus Buy?* often gets asked, "Isn't it hypocritical to ask people to pay money to see a film promoting anticonsumerism?" He responds, "No, but it is ironic."

Labels like *emergent, evangelical*, and even *Christian* can be helpful points of reference, provided one doesn't take the label, turn it into a designer logo, and market the product as if it's more important than Christ. In particular, how can anyone preach an anti-empire message while promoting oneself as a religious icon? This makes about as much sense as a Quaker owning a gun shop.

> *It is important to recognize though that not only those involved in the prosperity gospel but many of the rest of us in the church have uncritically embraced the Western dream as God's dream. Somehow we haven't realized that it enshrines individualism and the pursuit of self-interest, defining the good life in largely economic terms, as the individual pursuit of more — more economic upscaling, more choices and more experiences.*
>
> **Tom Sine,** *The New Conspirators*

During the 1980s, I was highly involved in both the Episcopal renewal and adult children of alcoholics movements. In my never-ending search for my next holy high, I consumed spirituality and recovery books like they were Christian crack. It was as if I couldn't get enough theological porn to really satisfy the cravings lodged deep inside my gut. After a while, the spiritual buzz wore off when I realized that, once you got beyond the flashy covers and the feel-good endorsements, most of these books delivered the same neat, prepackaged content. One can find similar product placements and promotions in any endeavor where there's a concerted effort to capitalize on a movement of the Spirit. Should these sparks get overhyped and mass-marketed, the light that attracted folks in the first place flickers out.

Despite the fact that holy hucksters pushing the latest faith fads provide religious satirists with a never-ending supply of material, my heart does go out to those who showed a lot of potential but sold out to the highest bidder. The promise of financial stability, coupled with the lure of power and fame, can present a really tempting piece of forbidden fruit that even Jesus struggled to resist (Matthew 4:1 – 11).

> *Money's a powerful thing, and it usually makes us alter our theologies to give it room.*
> **Peter Walker,** blogger, *emergingchristian.com*

One of the advantages of being a female religious satirist is that I seldom get even a peek at the garden of anti-Eden, let alone get presented with Judas-type opportunities to cash in at the expense of Christ. So I am not faced with the temptations that beset those mostly male authors/speakers who find themselves suddenly thrust into the spiritual spotlight and anointed as the new Messiah.

Being branded as the latest theological trend du jour reminds me of those disco divas circa 1980. When I covered HipHopEMass, I learned from Kurtis Blow that by the time *Saturday Night Fever* came out in 1977, they had already begun experimenting with what later became known as hip-hop. Disco still sold for a few years in the burbs, so one could still rake in a chunk of change playing to those who were desperate to be seen as part of the "in crowd."

However, disco divas were seen as a musical joke because the real spirit and the energy had moved on. In a touch of irony, now that rap has become a global gold mine, one finds old-school hip-hop artists like Kurtis rappin' as reverends. Time will tell if these moves are bling or Bible blessed.

> *But those who worship idols don't comprehend the cross.*
> **Larry Norman,** "Elvis Has Left the Building"

Don't get me started on those who become paid bloggers with bonuses for generating traffic to their site — or worse, their blogs morph into missional marketing machines paid for by their publishers. Somehow in this crass commercialization, establishing relationships takes a backseat to generating buzz and sales. Is their end goal to generate cha-ching or to foster an online community?

Even though I satirize spiritual sellouts, I get why actors, musicians, writers, visual artists, and other creatives decide to take the money and run. As a broke religious satirist, I've taken on tons of nonwriting gigs just so I could eat. At times, I've questioned why I didn't just hop on the biblical bandwagon and churn out faith fluff, bunny beatitudes, and righteous romance. I'd be living a lot more comfortably, that's for sure. Heck, I'd finally be in a position where I could actually help bankroll some very worthy ministries. But whenever I drift off into Commercial Christian® country, the thought of Jesus coming back to earth and turning the tables on me shakes me back into reality (Matthew 21:12 – 13; Mark 11:15 – 17; Luke 19:45 – 46; John 2:13 – 17).

Addendum: May 2009. Held in the midst of a global financial crisis, Book Expo 2009 proved to be more subdued, with most religious exhibitors either forgoing this event or downsizing their presence. Despite the reduction of book galleys and other freebies, fortunately one could still drink in a bestseller, courtesy of *The Shack* - branded water bottles.

The Writer

I have known that
Which many never know.
I have felt that
Which many never feel:
For this let me
Be Thankful.

Nancy Little, age sixteen. (Became Nancy Little Garrison at age eighteen and my mother a year later. Stopped writing. Died at the age of thirty-six.)

Walking the Thin Line

Andrew Jones, an internationally noted missiologist, aptly notes that the Jesus revolution in the United States was guitar driven. His observation brings to mind my childhood reflections of my late father's interactions with 1960s-era folk and psychedelic masses. In the mid-1980s, I picked up again on this trend by praising Jesus at St. Bart's and All Angels churches in New York City. During this time, I kept hearing about some amazing alternative worship services taking place in the United Kingdom, such as the Nine O'Clock Service and the Late Late Service. We all seemed to be experimenting with new forms of worship, though I didn't experience much cross-pollination across the pond.

According to Andrew:

> The disconnect in the U.S. between church culture and secular culture was much greater than in the UK. Radical change in worship forms were accepted into the church in the UK, but American churches closed the doors to new forms, or perhaps they thought their current forms were successful enough. The result is that emergent believers involved in emerging dance culture in the U.S. often bypassed the church and took their worship straight to the clubs, coffee shops, poetry slams, concerts, raves, galleries, and to whatever environment would accept it.

> Eventually, a number of us left the U.S. charismatic crowd when it began lifting hands in support of the political right — I prefer my church and state served separate, thank you.

Call it luck, fate, or the hand of God, but I reconnected with this global spirit when I reported on the HipHopEMass explosion happening up in the Bronx. One of the priests involved in this ministry introduced me to the work of Jonny Baker, one of the leaders of Grace, a Christian alternative worship community. Jonny and his buds like Andrew Jones and Steve Collins, a blogger who chronicles alternative worship / emerging church history, showed me how they had moved from planning worship services to forming communities. While my late father's forays into the Jesus revolution in the sixties seemed focused on finding inner peace, these folks sought to live out their faith by putting Christ's teachings into practice. These were the type of gatherings my heart had been longing for ever since the charismatic bubble burst. (In fact, I was introduced to U.S. emergent church icon Brian McLaren's work through Jonny — a bit of a backward way to connect to the U.S. emergent church scene, but then again, I'm Anglican, not postevangelical.)

THE EVOLUTION OF A WORSHIPPER

I prayed for the day when I could afford an extended trek to the United Kingdom and really immerse myself in this world that I had been experiencing online. In the summer of 2007, my dream became a reality when I was invited to speak at Greenbelt, an international social justice and arts festival.

By now, I'd learned from my treks to various places how to create tiny pockets of sacred space, even in the midst of Christian chaos. But I felt I really hadn't taken the advice given in *The Art of Pilgrimage* to move "from mindless to mindful, soulless to soulful travel. The difference may be subtle or dramatic; by definition it is life changing."

Although I had written a book that highlights a range of Christian communities and I live in a city of over eight million people, I was churchless. After the Iraq War broke out, I left a politically charged cathedral setting because the Bush-bashing from the pulpit only added to my pain. Afterward, I flirted with Catholicism, participated in forming an outreach service at a Lutheran church, tried to help launch an emergent cohort, and frequented a biweekly Episcopal contemporary praise service. After Pope Benedict was elected, the Lutheran church service veered off in a direction that didn't speak to me, the cohort deconstructed, and the Episcopal service closed shop. My job kept me on the road, sampling different worship experiences, so I remained a quasi-active churchgoer. But I didn't have a place I could call a spiritual home.

Since I was in this transitional state, my pilgrim guide Kurt Neilson encouraged me to ask myself a few key questions: What am I really seeking in these communities? How will I respond if my questions change? Am I ready to be surprised by the answers? Armed with these questions and a heart nearly ready to burst with excitement, I boarded my plane and headed across the pond.

Bend It Like Becket

Pre-Greenbelt, I took a mini-pilgrimage to Canterbury. As much as I'd like to replicate Chaucer's *Canterbury Tales* trek, no can do.

According to legend, his characters traveled along what is now the main A2, a major six-lane highway. I suspect those who try to traverse this road could end up as roadkill.

I settled for traveling to Canterbury via Continental Airlines, Gatwick Express, BritRail, and taxi. The Tempest-Moggs served as my tour guides for this part of the pilgrimage. They knew my father back in the early 1970s, when he helped them found Warnborough College. This college was based originally near Oxford as a place for American students to come and study abroad but has since moved to Canterbury. So, while I was traveling solo, I wasn't really all alone as I started my journey.

First stop, the Cathedral Gate Hotel. This quaint English B&B located next to the arch entrance to Canterbury Cathedral provided me with bare-bone amenities, the requisite overstuffed English tabby, and a bishop's-eye view of this stunning spire structure. A Shakespearean-style Starbucks sits nestled immediately below the hotel. Something tells me Chaucer & Co. did their mythical trek without the benefit of a Half-Caf No-Foam Venti Cap, though they clearly were in good spirits.

But Chaucer was by no means the first pilgrim to lay claim to this sacred spot. That honor goes to St. Augustine of Canterbury. This English saint should not be confused with Saint Augustine of Hippo, the notorious sinner who became a mighty saint. In 597 CE, Augustine of Canterbury and his Christian crew invaded this country at the request of Pope Gregory I. Apparently they dispensed with Gregory's instruction to be gentle and receptive to the Celts already present in Britain and tried to annihilate the Celtic embodiments of Christianity.

Throughout Canterbury and Kent, ancient churches stand as living testaments to Augustine's actions. Their soil speaks and creaks with the blood of martyrs and missionaries.

Dilapidated St. Augustine's Abbey remains in ruins, though one can find worship services at St. Martin's Church (597 CE), the oldest parish church in England still in use. By comparison, St. Dunstan's Church, built about four hundred years later, looked brand-spanking new.

I first entered Canterbury Cathedral to join a few brave souls down in the crypt for Morning Prayer and Holy Eucharist. "This is my body" takes on an added significance when one partakes of Communion while surrounded by row upon row of dead dudes.

While many famous folks remain entombed inside these hallowed halls, no one knows where St. Thomas Becket's body is buried. According to historical accounts, King Henry VIII took a break from his marital mania to despoil Becket's memorial. Some historians speculate that the body was burned, then the ashes placed in a cannon and fired over Canterbury. Given Henry's Tudor tirades, who knows?

But one can pray at the very spot where Becket kicked the bucket. A simple kneeler stands across from the door where four knights charged the cathedral on December 29, 1170. On the alleged orders of King Henry II, they murdered the praying archbishop of Canterbury. Seems the king banished Becket because he wouldn't let the crown run royal roughshod over the church. After a bit of pope play (this is pre-Reformation England after all), Becket returned to England to the cheers of an adoring public. Supposedly, the miffed majesty asked the now-infamous rhetorical question, "Will no one rid me of this turbulent priest?" thus proving that at times the sword can kick the pen to pieces.

After I knelt down, I tried to say a prayer, but the jagged cross sculpture that commemorates this unholy piece of religious history stared straight through me. I couldn't stop squirming, and yet Becket was able to pray in his own garden of Gethsemane, knowing full well the king could do away with him at any moment.

Once the quiet took over, I could really start to feel the presence of the evil that was done in this room. Thank goodness for incoming tourist traffic that broke this terrifying silence before I started channeling T. S. Eliot. Knowing my luck, instead of the eloquence of *Murder in the Cathedral*, I'd start reciting from his book *Old Possum's Book of Practical Cats*.

On my way out, I passed by a souvenir stand. They didn't offer such imaginary confections as Becket biscuits or Monty Python-esque Black Knight figurines, though one can buy archbishop teddy bears, "pilgrims riding to Canterbury" silk ties, and replica medieval pilgrim tokens depicting the murder of St. Thomas Becket. Upon leaving the cathedral, one could frequent the Thomas Becket pub for a shot of Royal Crown.

To the town's credit, Canterbury tends to rein in the really tacky bits. If anything, Christian bookstores veer on the dry side, as though they're awaiting a visit from the characters in Monty Python's "The Bishop" or "The Spanish Inquisition" sketches to whip them into spiritual shape. But the bishop brigade wouldn't start until summer 2008, when Lambeth happens. As religious satirists are not issued press passes to this international gathering of bishops, I've never seen this Anglican extravaganza up close and personal. But by all news accounts, every eight years these relatively modest towns turn a bright sea of purple when bishops and other dignitaries descend in droves.

I did tour Kent University, the place where these almighty Anglicans will do the bulk of their blessings and bickerings. Somehow I expected something more Oxfordesque and Anglican, but this place looked like a cookie-cutter community college. My tour of Kent concluded with a stop at Warnborough College. This institution remains my father's only remaining testament to his work as a professor and priest. I don't remember where in western North Carolina my parents are buried. Frankly, I don't feel a pull to visit the gravesites that mark that period of my life when I descended into some dark-night-of-the-soul sinkhole after losing both my parents before my seventeenth birthday. But visiting the plaque dedicated to my parents served as a visible marker that even though Dad died in a pit of darkness, there was a brief period when his light shone.

Refreshed and over my jet lag, I boarded the train and headed out to the Cheltenham Racecourse. In my excitement about finally going to the Greenbelt Experience, I forgot all the pressing questions Kurt Neilson had told me to ponder.

Going Green for God

I had been dreaming of Greenbelt ever since Jonny Baker connected me to the global emerging church scene. When this Christian music and arts festival with a strong social justice edge launched in 1974, about two thousand people showed up. Adopting Karl Barth's approach of taking the Bible in one hand and the newspaper in the other, they have maintained a tradition of inviting artists and activists with a global perspective. Currently, close to twenty thousand kindred spirits gather together from the UK, Europe, and beyond for an event that has become an international meeting place for Christians on the fringe with a vast array of music, talks, performing arts, visual arts, and other intergenerational programming.

> *Greenbelt is part of my mental furniture.*
> **Archbishop Rowan Williams**

I arrived in Greenbelt the day before the event began so I could survey the scene and get my bearings. A group of California-style Jesus hippies with British accents greeted me as they scurried around like church mice trying to make the magic happen by Friday afternoon.

Eventually I hooked up with Dave King, the kind soul who arranged the details for my speaking gig. He connected me with my escort, a chipper older woman who delighted in showing me around. After her tour, I had my bearings.

All was well until I showed up for my first event. When I went to sit with someone I thought I knew, I immediately discovered that online buddies don't always translate into real-world relationships. I confess to having some rather obnoxious and ornery traits — hanging out with a satirist isn't everyone's cup of tea — but I thought I'd be grabbing beers with a few virtual friends. Instead, I watched them go off clubbing with their post-Christian clique. Sometimes it seems that high school never ends.

Common sense would dictate that I should focus on the many people who greeted me with smiles and blow off those few "friends" who acted like they were too cool for school. I wish I was that sane and practical, but that's not how I'm wired. I've read enough recovery literature to realize how as the oldest child, I became the adult in the Garrison household at way too early an age. The slew of self-help experts wouldn't hit the airwaves and bestseller lists for another decade. Hence, I didn't realize how growing up with alcoholic parents who were never "there" impacted me. Also, I had no clue that many of my peers also became collateral damage as a result of our parents' quests to "find themselves" through drugs and alcohol. We were all together in the same classroom or youth group — but all alone.

Years of spiritual direction, therapy, and other such tools have uncovered my fears of abandonment, a fact I prefer to keep well hidden underneath thick layers of self-sufficiency. Such armor enables me to laugh off the stones and arrows that get thrown at a satirist, though sometimes, like this first night at Greenbelt, a spike pierces through when I find myself isolated in a sea of people. Like a bit of bad beef, my adult-child-of-alcoholics tendencies kicked in full force and gave me a massive spiritual stomachache.

Unfortunately, I'd been so busy writing that my prayer life had fallen into the toilet once again. Whenever I get too disconnected from God, I always end up with a religious rash.

I woke up the next morning still scratching myself and wondering if anyone would show up for my 10:00 a.m. talk. Fortunately, over a hundred folks came to sit and sweat indoors for a chat about religious satire, followed by a serving of scripture candy. Relieved to have delivered my first talk in foreign territory, I strolled around and sampled some of the social justice booths and art displays.

Finally I connected with Jon Birch, the cartoonist behind some rather twisted creations over at "The Ongoing Adventures of ASBO Jesus." For us non-Brits, Jon decodes the meaning behind his site's name: "An 'asbo' is an 'anti-social behaviour order.' The courts here award them to people who are deemed to be constant trouble in their neighbourhoods — presumably according to their neighbours!" Through the online community that's formed around commenting about his cartoons, I've discovered a group of broken buddies who help keep me connected and grounded.

During Greenbelt, Jon and Jonny Baker relaunched an amazing artists' collective aptly named Proost, which means "cheers" in Dutch. This collaborative selection of worship resources celebrates the contributions of artists without elevating them to the status of spiritual superstars where they get put on a pedestal and become objects of worship.

Seeing these guys together reminded me a bit of watching old Dean Martin and Jerry Lewis films, with Jonny playing the sophisticated straight man to the more puckish  Jon. (Only I doubt Dean Martin wore surfing shorts, and I've never seen Jerry Lewis with a soul patch.) Like Martin and Lewis, Baker and Birch melded together to form this creative combo exploding with a kinetic energy to produce some unexpected yet magical moments.

At the party for Proost, I got to connect with my online buddy

Andrew Jones (a.k.a. Tall Skinny Kiwi). I wish I'd had more time to chill with him, though I am pleased to report that he is as kind and sweet as he is tall and skinny.

On Sunday afternoon, I finally met G. P. Taylor. When his book *Wormwood* was released in the States, I interviewed him for *The Wittenburg Door* and found him to be an absolute hoot over the telephone. I wanted to explore his days as the road manager for the Sex Pistols, though he preferred to focus on his present career as a bestselling Christian author. (In the UK, his children's books rival J. K. Rowling's Harry Potter franchise in terms of popularity.)

Except for a few major authors and a couple of invited Americans, most of the folks in the Greenbelt lineup aren't very familiar voices to U.S. audiences. That's because Greenbelt attracts a wide range of internationally known Christian leaders who focus on building up communities instead of promoting themselves on the author/speaker circuit. Here they have a strong model in Jesus Christ. The only recorded instance of Jesus actually writing occurred during the incident of the woman caught in adultery (John 8:2 – 11). If what he etched into the desert sand was deemed vitally important, like the Lord's Prayer or the Beatitudes, then one of the gospel writers would have noted what he wrote. Heck, he used his finger; for all we know, Jesus could have been doodling.

If, when traveling, all one does is hang out with pastors and speakers who have book deals, it's like staying at some corporate hotel chain and eating at chain restaurants and then harboring the delusion that one has really experienced a new place. I say this as someone who's been guilty of chomping down on faith fast food. I used to regard those with published products as "religious experts," but after enduring one too many cases of the religious runs, so to speak, I decided to move beyond the glare of the Gospel Arches.

Off in the corners, I found people living out in a myriad of ways what it means to "be the church" in this post-Christian (secularized) culture where no more than, say, 10 percent of the population goes to church each Sunday. Slowly I began to meet the locals, talk with them, and worship with their communities.

During Greenbelt, I sampled worship that ranged from a high Anglo-Catholic mass to God gunk, and I even tried Communion by numbers a few times. Jonny Baker, along with fellow members from Grace, devised an interactive service where worshipers gathered in small groups. A priest presided over the Eucharist prayer as we administered Communion to each other step-by-step.

To the untrained eye, Greenbelt could look like another hippie-dippy peace concert. A few bits of performance art did veer toward the delusional end of the spectrum, and yes, I confess to being on a major spiritual high, so I'm definitely theologically tripping. Still, these services seemed more real than many of the megawatt and watered-down worship services I experienced back in the States.

I confess to a sweet tooth, so I can often gauge worship by the amount of sugar that goes into the service. For example:

Prosperity preachers = a five-pound bag of processed white sugar

Predestination preaching = 144,000 servings of milk 'n' honey

Megachurch PowerPoint praise band = a box of Splenda®

A U.S. Emergent Church™ conference = a few packets of faux equal (that no-brand stuff that's designed to fool you into thinking it's Equal®)

Typical mainline church service = half a packet of Sweet & Low®

Let's not get into those churches that dish out salt blocks in lieu of sugar cubes.

Fortunately, I've been to enough services that serve raw natural sugar, so I still have hope — unfortunately, they're almost all in the UK. Why does God want me on the other side of the pond when my spiritual sensibilities remain more in tune with the UK? I can really identify with Jonah's disgust with the great city of Nineveh right about now (Jonah 4).

After I gave my second talk satirizing the New Atheists, I circled the site one more time. By now I was so into the Greenbelt groove that I could have stayed and soaked in this spiritual sun forever. But the festival was over. Time for this pilgrim to move on.

Thames Talking

After Greenbelt, I connected with a first cousin who had married and relocated to Thame, a hamlet situated near London and Oxford. We hadn't seen each other since her wedding some fifteen years earlier, though we communicated in bits and pieces via email. Most of my family pushes daisies these days, so I try to connect with those few remaining relatives who don't view the Garrisons as black sheep.

Shortly before I embarked on this journey, I learned my cousin's dad had cancer that could be treated but not cured. Once again, I was doing the pre-death dance, a family ritual I've repeated so often that I know the steps by heart; but I'm so rhythmically challenged that the dancing never gets any easier. We talked a bit about her father's illness, though the bulk of our time was spent swapping photos, catching up on family news, and basically getting to know each other again.

I was also there to connect with the Rev. Dr. Steve Croft, who at that time headed up Fresh Expressions of Church. While this name might bring to mind visions of some kind of holy hygiene product, FE of C actually represents a major initiative by the Church of England, endorsed by the archbishop of Canterbury, to create a mixed economy of church whereby new ways of being church engage alongside more traditional styles of church. *Mission* and *money* tend to be two words seldom uttered in Episcopal circles, but here Anglicans seek to embrace a mission agenda as part of the church's role in the contemporary British context.

Rev. Croft and I met in Oxford at Martyrs' Memorial, a spire-like structure that commemorates Bloody Mary's Bishops BBQ.

She flame-broiled Bishops Latimer and Ridley in 1555, followed by a hand-cut steak a la Archbishop Cranmer the following year. (Truth be told, the English have never been known for their fine cuisine.) We chatted over lunch about how the UK and U.S. Anglican churches can interact with each other. Such connections have started to send sparks across both sides of the pond, with pioneers like the Rev. Karen Ward, abbess of Church of the Apostles in Seattle and director of Episcopal Village, seeking creative strategies to support, resource, and fund "fresh expression" U.S. Episcopal church plants and missions.

Following our too-brief meeting, Rev. Croft directed me toward an iron cross set in the pavement outside Balliol College, which marks the spot where Cranmer croaked. Would Cranmer have given the thumbs-up to my assessment that mixing empire and church tends to produce a toxic theological cocktail? What would the man who departed from Roman Catholic liturgies to craft a prayer book that would be accessible to the common man think about how Anglicans interpret these rites in the twenty-first century?

Afterward, I soaked in a bit of C. S. Lewis. Rather than booking a prepackaged not-so-pastoral pilgrimage, I strolled around Magdalen College, stopped by Blackwell's Bookshop for some tea, and walked along the bank of the River Thames. I hadn't been to Oxford since the early 1980s when I attended Warnborough College for a semester, but yet the city felt familiar to me.

The Anti-C. S. Lewis Shop

My day ended on a high note, thanks to a Celtic-inspired service and potluck supper in the park led by Ian Adams of the mayBe Community. At first, I almost missed mayBe because I expected something more "churchy." Every time I turned a corner in C. S. Lewisland, I was surrounded by spires and steeples. But if you knocked on the church doors, you'd discover that, except for the tourist trade, hardly anyone was home anymore.

Despite New Atheist guru and Oxford don Richard Dawkins's delusion that religion is dead in the UK and other "civilized" countries, step back from the prominent cathedrals and churches and you'll find people gathering in houses, pubs, and other public spaces. I wonder what Dawkins would say if I asked him to leave his ivory tower and help me find the mayBe community. Something tells me that his response would be unprintable.

After wandering around for a bit, I found about fifty people playing in the park and realized this must be mayBe. No spires but plenty of space.

Ian gently called the group together for a simple Celtic prayer service. Through mayBe's gentle spirit, I felt the presence of the living Christ speaking to me through this ancient earth.

> *Touching the truth with our minds alone is not enough. We are also made to touch it with our bodies. I think this is why Christian tradition clings to the reality of resurrection, even when no one can explain it to anyone else's satisfaction.*
> **Barbara Brown Taylor,** *An Altar in the World*

If I didn't know that Ian was an ordained Anglican priest, I'd have no clue "who was in charge." Such is often the nature of these UK communities. These leaders tend to see themselves as facilitators or curators who work in the background, similar to a DJ, rather than placing themselves front and center. Hence, their gatherings represent an expression of the life of the community rather than an event led by a charismatic leader.

I'd been away long enough from the ungodly glitter of Americana Christianity™ that I could see with greater clarity the glimpses of God that peek through the Christian cracks whenever two or three are gathered in his name. Seeing these communities in action gave me hope that we can find ways to remove the evangelical excesses that have come to define Jesus, USA — and let the risen Christ shine. I had to exert some effort to find mayBe. So perhaps I am not looking hard enough for similar U.S.-based communities.

The next day, I continued my stroll around Oxford. Then I

headed over to the Church Mission Society (CMS) to chat with Jonny Baker about how to bring Proost UK and the Anglican ethos over to the United States. When we took up the topic of missions, I kept wondering how we can interact with the local Christian churches and organizations that are already present in a given area. What prevents U.S. churches from learning from other cultures instead of showing up to "minister" to them, as though their methods and money represent the only way to "do church"? I left Jonny loaded down with more questions than answers. Thank God for email and blogs, as these conversations need to continue.

I realized I should have booked more time in Oxford, as I felt I was just starting to connect with Ian, Jonny, and my cousin when it was time to depart. But Ireland was calling.

Skating on Thin Space

I departed Oxford for a daylong train/ferry ride to Ireland, per Kurt Neilson's request that I set foot on Irish soil. After one nudge too many from Kurt, I decided to book short jaunts to Glendalough and Kildare instead of sampling a few of Ireland's world-renowned fly-fishing spots. He thought I needed to walk on these particular patches, adding that Irish saints like Kevin and Brigid embodied this concept of pilgrimage, where their entire lives became one sacred journey that connected this world to the next.

In particular, Kurt talked to me about "thin space," that imaginary veil that separates this world from the next, where we can almost reach out and touch the angels. I have a taste of this sometimes when I fly-fish or kayak; with each cast or paddle stroke, I can feel pieces of me melt into the horizon. I'm no longer observing nature but am part of the picture. If I allow myself the time to really be still and listen, the line between where I end and nature begins becomes obliterated in a swirl of impressionist brushstrokes.

After I unloaded my bags, I uploaded Sinead O'Connor's *Theology* CD onto my MP3 player. Her soothing yet haunting lyrics put me in the right frame of mind for setting forth on Celtic sod.

The next morning, I left for Glendalough via a private bus

service named after the venerable St. Kevin, abbot of Glendalough. This sixth-century monk founded the monastery of Glendalough and left his faithful fingerprints all over these hills. After I toured the ruins of Monastic City and walked around the two lakes (*gleann dá locha* means literally "glen of the two lakes"), the touristy chatter started to get on my nerves. I almost hopped on the afternoon bus, until I remembered that my hostel room was already charged to my credit card.

Stuck in Glendalough, I set out for a late-afternoon hike beyond the two lakes toward the ruins of an abandoned mining village. Rows of purple heather greeted me with pine trees serving as an umbrella to shade me from the sun. Finally I got to sample paradise almost all by myself.

En route, I glanced out at the hole in the rock called "St. Kevin's Bed," a seven-by-three-foot cave that apparently was shown to him by an angel. Like other good hermits, he lived off the land, consuming herbs and fish. Legend has it that as part of his prayer routine, he would stand in ice-cold water up to his neck.

While stories abound recounting Kevin's unbridled kindness toward animals, this nature lover had a major dislike of women. According to rumor, he dealt with an amorous woman by pushing her into a bed of nettles.

As I walked, the sky opened up and baptized me, in typical Irish fashion. I literally soaked in St. Kevin. Every time I took a step, I went squish-squish. Rather than rant and rave, I turned this into a prayer mantra of sorts, courtesy of the Jesus Prayer.

> Lord Jesus, Son of the living God
> (step, squish-squish),
> Have mercy on me, a sinner
> (step, squish-squish).
> (Rinse and repeat.)

The rain drenched my body but fed my soul. With each step, I could feel myself opening up more and more and more — and then God let it rip. A hailstorm of his tears poured into me. I joined in God's joyful lament. We both cried, for I had been apart from the

Father for far too long. At least for now, this prodigal daughter had returned.

On the way home, a rainbow frown graced the sky. No, I didn't rattle off strings of leprechaun pot o' gold jokes, though I could have sworn I saw the shadow of some crusty old coot staring at me from St. Kevin's Bed. Now I get why Kevin's name means "he of blessed birth." It took a really good dunking in his country for my prayer life to be reborn.

After I dried myself off, I left for dinner and my first taste of authentic Guinness. I took a mobile phone picture of my pint and emailed Kurt a toast. So far, his assessment proved to be right on target.

The next morning, I bought a trail map and set out to meet the Wicklow Mountains up close and personal. As I surveyed the scenery, I could see the pine-covered, mossy mountains off in the distance, grinning at me like a Cheshire cat daring me to set out on one of the treacherous climbs not recommended for solo travelers.

"You know you want it."

"If you thought the Upper Lake was remarkable, you ain't seen nuttin' yet."

The adventurer in me contemplated climbing my own personal Mount Everest, but I let my head win this battle and chose a clearly marked trail that would take me to the site of St. Kevin's cell.

Once I got embedded deep into the purple heather, I took off my shoes. With each step, the moss encircled my feet, as though to provide me with a pair of nature's own slippers. Now I see why there's no talk of Jesus in Celtic circles. I could feel him tingling beneath my toes. Passing waterfall after waterfall, I could see Christ's eyes in the water winking at me, daring me to join him in his dance. I accepted the challenge and skipped myself silly. What a way to pray.

Following a full day of prayer-play, I ventured into the neighboring town to receive Communion at St. Kevin's Church. I returned to the hostel exhausted and eager for a sound night's sleep.

Unfortunately, I was kept awake all night by some highly rude bunkmates who had clearly soaked in some different spirits. (No singles were available at the only hostel or I would have paid a bit extra for a solid night's sleep.) I would have crawled into Kevin's cave, except the entrance is closed to the public.

Double dog tired, I got out of bed around 5:00 a.m., grumpy as all get-out. Unable to sleep, I figured I might as well grab some breakfast and catch the first bus back to Dublin. No one else was around, so I had Monastic City all to myself. A stone wall beckoned me to have a seat and watch the morning sun rise over the ruins.

The sky went from a midnight blue to a deep majestic purple. For a few brief moments, these dull gray Celtic crosses turned a bright shiny silver, as though the ghosts of Glendalough rose up to bid me good-bye. God's Galilean sun God-smacked me again. I waved to these ancient saints and skipped myself silly all over again.

Thank God I couldn't get a lick of sleep or I would have missed this opportunity to play on nature's trampoline and join in God's cosmic circus.

Brigid or Bust

Next on the agenda was a short train ride to Kildare for my encounter with the infamous St. Brigid. This mythical figure morphed over the years to include both Brigids — the pre-Christian goddess and the historic Christian. After founding Kildare Abbey, a double monastery for nuns and monks, in 470 CE, Brigid wielded considerable power equivalent to that of a bishop. However, despite her increasing sphere of influence, she kept her feet on the ground. Sounds like a woman I'd like to know.

After I got off the train in Kildare, I set off for my appointment with one of the sisters from Solas Bhride (a Christian community centre for Celtic spirituality in the spirit of Brigid of Kildare). I almost walked by the nondescript suburban house that houses this center because I was expecting a quaint stone convent. After a bit of prayer, tea, and a short tour of the center, I bought a booklet outlining the pilgrimage and set out on my way.

Kurt proved to be spot-on in his assessment of Glendalough. But the graffiti and grime in Kildare made me question his spiritual sanity a tad. Nothing says "You go, Brigid" like a montage of poorly drawn naked men etched on a wall facing St. Brigid's Cathedral (Anglican), a thirteenth-century gem of a church. (Yes, Ireland remains predominately Catholic, but since the crown was in charge post-Reformation, they oversaw the cathedrals, thus demonstrating they were the alpha Anglicans on the block.) A pair of welcoming hands served as door handles for St. Brigid's Parish Church (Catholic), but this newer joint built in 1833 was definitely closed. So much for welcoming the pilgrim.

After passing by some famed abbey ruins, I stumbled upon St. Brigid's Well. When a woman started smoking in this somewhat confined space, I almost left, but then I decided that would be very unpilgrimlike of me.

A set of five prayer stones paved the way to the well. My pilgrimage book listed a prayer for each stone: Woman of the Land, Peacemaker, Friend of the Poor, Hearthwarmer, and Woman of Contemplation. This sounded more than slightly New Agey, but I decided to give it a go. As I mumbled each prayer in order, I felt like a complete devotional dope. I didn't have an epiphany, but I was able to stop and offer a prayer and a few coins at the well for God to release me from my anger and anxiety. That's a start, I guess.

On the way back to the train, I stopped by two twelfth-century abbeys in ruins and a sign that read "Bull Performance Testing Center." Given her ability to cut through the BS, something tells me Brigid could tackle these bulls. No problem.

After Brigid was buried in a tomb inside her abbey church following her death around 525 CE, her skull was extracted and carried to Igreja de São João Baptista in Lisbon, Portugal, where it remains today. Eventually the rest of her body was shipped to Downpatrick, where she joined the two other patron saints of Ireland, Patrick of

Ireland and Columba of Iona. But her soul remains embedded in this soil, still speaking to many pilgrims loud and clear. After all, this is the spot that moved Kurt to tears.

Then why didn't I feel anything? This major force of nature and icon of feminist power sounds like someone I'd fall in love with immediately if I were to meet her in person. She could be the incredibly cool best friend I never had — you know, the kind of person who makes you popular by association. Yet when I walked in her shoes, I didn't connect with her spirit. Meanwhile, back in Glendalough, my prayer life got rejuvenated by a guy who would have dismissed me with a wave of his hand. Then again, while I wish I could possess Brigid's remarkable leadership skills, Kevin and I probably have more in common than I might like to admit. We're both single-minded in our solitary pursuits and can be quite irritating at times — *popular* is not a word I'd use to describe either one of us.

I'm not crazy about the fact that I fell in love with such a prickly hermit. But once again, Christ's radical love dissolved those man-made barriers that too often separate Christians from each other.

My Mecca

Sometimes as Christians, we act oh so holy. I, for one, can get my head so far in the clouds that I need a swift kick in the pants to bring me back to earth. A few days touring Dublin — Jonathan Swift's stomping ground — should keep me well grounded.

I played tourist for a day, thanks to the kind folks at Dublin Tourism who provided me with a Dublin pass. Celtic monks might have produced the Book of Kells on the isolated island of Iona, but the flock of tourists pecking at me somehow took away from the magic of seeing these masterpieces. As much as I enjoyed trolling around the Old Jameson Distillery, the Guinness Storehouse, and the Dublin Writers Museum, my heart began pounding when I entered St. Patrick's Cathedral. For it is here that my hero and religious satirist extraordinaire Jonathan Swift served as Dean of the Cathedral.

While Ireland remains heavily Roman Catholic, the Church of

Ireland (Anglican) oversees both Christ Church Cathedral and St. Patrick's Cathedral. No wonder Swift was so cranky. Being an Anglican clergyman (a.k.a. the royal representative) in Roman Catholic Ireland was no pastoral picnic, even if one did get to be dean of the country's national cathedral.

As I read up on Swift, I realized on some level that we're similar souls. I doubt this Irishman shared my penchant for Single Malt Scotch, though we both found ourselves ensconced within an institutional structure that, frankly, doesn't suit our personalities.

Now, Swift might have wielded a satirical sword, but he also walked the walk. During his tenure as Dean of the Cathedral, he built an almshouse for elderly women who were unable to support themselves. Also, Swift despised seeing mentally ill people put on public display as though they were circus freaks. Upon his death, he left a fortune of twelve thousand pounds to found a hospital for those suffering from mental illness.

These accomplishments aren't chronicled in the ostentatious display of Swift memorabilia. But one can find items such as his table, a marble bust, his chalice, copies of *A Modest Proposal* and other works under glass, a cast of his skull, and his death mask. I wonder how Swift would respond to this devotional display of his personal artifacts and body parts?

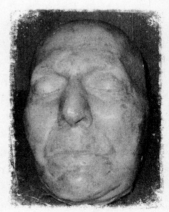
Swift at Sleep

When I passed by Swift's grave, I did a double take. Now, I'm well aware of the unholy hanky-panky that has plagued the church from the get-go. But how many clergymen get buried in a cathedral next to a woman who is not their wife? My hero received a Christian burial in a cathedral alongside his much younger "lady friend" Esther Johnson (Stella). When I read his poems "On Stella's Birthday" and "Stella's Distress," I didn't realize that Swift met Stella when he tutored this teen as part of his duties as private secretary to Sir William Temple.

His epitaph reads:

Here is laid the body of Jonathan Swift, Doctor of Divinity, Dean of this Cathedral Church, where fierce indignation can no longer rend the heart. Go, traveler, and imitate if you can this earnest and dedicated champion of liberty.

This call to action stopped my snickering in its tracks. Lesson learned.

Belfast Blues

Next I trekked up to Belfast for a few meetings. During the two-hour train ride, I felt a chill in the hot autumn air. Presbyterian prim and proper quickly replaced the Celtic charm that I had come to love.

My research into the global emerging and underground church scene backed up these perceptions. England, Wales, and (to a lesser extent) Scotland have a considerably more "secularized" culture in which the church is marginalized than Northern Ireland does. In Belfast and the surrounding environs, most people have in their family background some kind of Christian formation, whereas the vast majority of the population in the rest of the UK cannot claim the same. There's a much greater similarity between the religious culture of North America and Northern Ireland than there is between Northern Ireland and the rest of the United Kingdom.

These observations were borne out when I toured several Christian bookstores in Belfast. These stores carried roughly the same products that one finds in any evangelical bookstore in the United States. I could not find similar bookstores elsewhere in the UK.

Once I finished two of my meetings, I tried to connect with an experiential-artists collective marketed in the States as the epitome of post-Christian cool. But for some reason or another, our timing was off. Sometimes these things just happen. So we never got to meet in person. As I walked around the Belfast town centre, pondering what I might do with my free time, Kurt's penetrating questions cut through me like a knife: What am I really seeking in these communities? How will I respond if my questions change? Am I ready to be surprised by the answers?

Surprised isn't exactly the word I'd use when I found myself stuck in Belfast. *Alone.* C. S. Lewis might have been born in Belfast, but the person working the counter at the tourist bureau had no information about any of his haunts. So I couldn't revisit Lewisland, as I did back at Oxford. I took a short river cruise, but I had an inkling the water wouldn't work its usual magic on me when the woman selling tickets was also hawking Titanic merchandise. Somehow I didn't see myself wearing a T-shirt with the cheeky catchphrase "Titanic: She Was Alright When She Left Here!"

I knew there must be glimmers of light hidden somewhere. But without a guide to show me the way, I was lost. Whatever luck of the Irish I had amassed ran out. Everyone from the waitress who threw food in my general direction like I was a pig lining up at a trough to the people who poked me in the street served as painful reminders that I should get out of here. This ugly American didn't belong.

The rowdy hostel guests rendered me unable to get some much-needed rest. Sleep deprivation plus total isolation equals recollections of childhood taunts — you're ugly, useless, undesirable. Even the still voices that usually comforted me when I travel alone were silent. Not even the soil spoke to me. The thin line I encountered in Ireland that connected me from this world to the next snapped.

Walking around the city, I spotted churches looking down at me with a Dobsonesque air, as though they dared to discipline me for some unknown transgression. I saw crosses aplenty but no sign of the living Christ. I knew God was present here because I'd heard about the groundbreaking initiatives being implemented by some of the peace churches in Northern Ireland. But again, without anyone around to point me in the right direction, I didn't know how to find these folks on such short notice.

My stomach spiraled. Down, down, down, veering toward no-man's-land — that place with no name where I crashed the day my mother died and I became an "orphan." I vowed to myself that I would never go there — ever, ever again. Yet I felt myself suddenly hightailing it with the brakes busted. I got out my BlackBerry and tried to figure out who would be up at this hour. I came across the number of a close friend who's enough of a night owl that I assumed she'd be up. Fortunately, she answered the phone.

"You're in Belfast," she said after I dumped my lousy mood on her.

"Yeah, so ..."

She probably shrugged. Her voice certainly indicated that I was not seeing the obvious. "What did you expect?" she asked.

"Huh?"

"You're in a place that probably hasn't healed enough to welcome the total stranger."

She brought me back to earth. I still felt totally isolated, but I knew I wasn't really all alone.

I could have kicked myself for not listening to my gut. Sometimes I'm too smart for my own good. This trek to Belfast served as a painful reminder of how easily I can get off track when I lose my footing on the pilgrim path and try to catch a philosophical paper tiger by its tail by trying to cover the newest shiny theological toy instead of following the living Christ.

After boarding the 6:00 a.m. ferry, I ordered a Baileys on the rocks and toasted myself for making it through the night. After a two-hour ferry ride, I reveled in a daylong train excursion from Scotland to London. I tried to sleep, but instead of counting sheep, I kept seeing images of Monty Pythonesque lambs flying, imploding, and doing other dastardly deeds I dare not mention. Freud would have had a field day playing inside my mind.

Lovin' London

By the time I got to London, I was beat but refreshed. I let myself oversleep, so I missed out on touring Westminster Abbey and St. Paul's Cathedral, though I did attend both churches' Evensongs along with a large collection of tourists and a motley crew of locals.

With the exception of the London Eye, a steel Ferris wheel monstrosity that gives the city a rather bizarre circus feel, the sights of London retained a familiar air. Somehow this city felt like home again, even though I hadn't been there for decades. So when a few online friends weren't able to connect with me, I got a bit bummed, but nowhere close to getting the Belfast blues again.

Having lost track of time, I had to make a mad dash over to St. Mary's Church, Ealing, where the Grace community held their biweekly Saturday evening service. Since I've used this emerging community's liturgies and Jonny Baker's music for my own personal devotions, this was my one must-see stop. Steve Collins's warm welcome and Jonny Baker's ambient music, coupled with the video projections and beanbag chairs, made this church sanctuary feel like — well, like "home."

Like a number of other UK communities I've met, the members of Grace inform the ethos of their gatherings by bringing in the technologies and media of their everyday lives — TV, video, iPods, computers, face-to-face conversations. They employ these tools not to create cool worship but so they can connect with each other, using those particular pieces that speak to them. Instead of eschewing culture, communities like Grace seek to follow the example of Jesus, who both immersed himself in the culture of his day and challenged it. Each group is shaped by the uniqueness of its specific setting; a community based in, say, London, Telford, or Oxford will take on the vibe of that particular city's cultural milieu.

That night's gathering reflected on the Rule of Life for the Grace community: create, participate, engage, and risk. During the service we gathered into small groups around cutout drawings of footprints. Then we were given a candle and asked to reflect on what prayers we needed for where we were going on our journey. Placing my candle on a set of feet, I prayed I would find the strength to walk with Christ without being quite so bowlegged.

Afterward, we gathered for a bit of wine, food, and fellowship. Worshiping with my online UK-based buddies reminded me of the need to connect with each other not only virtually but also face-to-face. The televangelists might claim that they can cure for cash through the TV, but all throughout his ministry Jesus healed people one touch at a time (Matthew 9:18–26; Mark 5:21–43; Luke 8:41–56). No matter how plugged-in we get, I can't hug my laptop.

And the ritual partaking of the Last Supper entails that we feed each other actual bread and wine.

I overslept again on Sunday, thus missing a morning alternative worship service in North London that was high on my to-do agenda. My pilgrim sensibilities kicked in before I could kick myself, reminding me that I need to just let what happens happen.

So I blew church — but I hit up the Tower of London. Talk about anti–emerging church.

In preparation for my mini-historical trek, I uploaded the soundtrack from *Spamalot* onto my MP3 player. Listening to how Sir Robin the Not-Quite-So-Brave-As-Sir-Lancelot personally wet himself at the Battle of Badon Hill put me in the right frame of mind to visit England's most infamous house of horrors.

I started out on a guided tour led by a gentleman dressed in regal robes. But after getting elbowed one time too many by some twittery tourist, I set out on my own.

This massive twenty-one-tower complex built by William the Conqueror shortly after he came into power in 1066 served a variety of functions, including a fortress against foreign attack, a repository for the crown jewels, and a refuge for the royal family in times of civil disorder. However, the Tower of London remains notorious as the site of some of England's bloodiest bits, a living testimony to the hell that happened when certain royals ruled the roost.

In recent years, the Tower underwent a thorough "out, damned spot!" removal program. The last execution at the Tower transpired when an eight-man firing squad shot Corporal Josef Jakobs in 1941, the same year that Hitler's Deputy Führer, Rudolf Hess, was held there briefly. Even the famous Bloody Tower now glistens in the golden sun. A pastoral patch on the Tower Green marks the spot where the more prominent prisoners, such as two of Henry VIII's wives (Anne Boleyn and Catherine Howard), lost their pretty heads. All that's left now are a few implements of torture ensconced in glass cases. Let's pray they stay that way.

After spending a day walking around the Tower of London, I managed to catch the last half of Church on the Corner's Sunday evening service. By then I was too pooped to pray, so I just sat there and soaked in a bit of the buzz left over from Greenbelt.

According to my calculations, I barely scratched the surface when it came to sampling UK church fare. Maybe I should make another foray into Ireland; surely some other saints would speak to me. I hadn't realized just how empty I was until I had my first real pint of Guinness after soaking in St. Kevin at Glendalough.

At this point I suspected I dipped a bit too much into the pilgrim spirits. As a visitor to these communities, I wasn't really experiencing the day-to-

Once again, Anne B. lost her pretty little head in the gift shop.

day bickerings that one finds in any ministerial endeavor. If I actually lived here, I'm sure once the "new church" smell wore off, I'd find some of the frustrations one finds among any group of people who gather together to explore what it means for them to follow Christ.

Still, I'm envious of those who are free to explore God in a post-Christian context sans any of the baggage that gets attached to being called an "American Christian." But I don't get a sense of God calling me to pick up and actually relocate. I do expect, based on the online relationships that transformed into real-time friends, that I'll be back again. And again. And again. Amen.

Balaam's Ass Rides Again

September 2007

Throughout my time in Israel, our guide kept telling us, "If you want to experience the real earth of the Holy Land, go to Jordan. The country hasn't been overdeveloped, and you can get a real sense of what the land felt like during biblical times." So when I received an invitation to go on a ten-day press trip to Jordan, I jumped at the chance.

I knew I'd made the right choice when I arrived at JFK Airport in New York City to catch my midnight flight to Amman, Jordan. The terminal was filled with families toting children, household goods, and even groceries, thus lending a friendly marketplace atmosphere to the airport. I chuckled to myself as I visualized a herd of goats joining this menagerie.

As I felt myself beginning to run through a list of stereotypes, I instead resolved to watch and learn as much as I could. I was about to embark on my first trip to a largely Muslim country; 92 per-

How (not) to experience the Holy Land

cent of Jordanians are Sunni Muslims, and approximately 6 percent are Christians (mostly of the Greek Orthodox variety, though one can find a smattering of other Catholic and Orthodox groups and a few Protestant denominations). This would be a pilgrimage of a different sort — a cultural pilgrimage, a journey enhanced by the fact we were visiting Jordan during the Islamic holy month of Ramadan.

After deplaning and getting through customs, we were taken to our hotel in Amman. The hotels required all their guests to go through a metal detector prior to entrance. Unlike my Bethlehem fiasco, I made it through every detector with nary a beep.

"Shukran." (Thank you.)

After a quick lunch, we had a half day of free time. I secured an appointment to meet with the kind folks at Habitat for Humanity Jordan. Since I volunteered off and on with Habitat in the United States, I wanted to learn how this Christian-based program operated overseas.

Another journalist asked to join me, so off we went. Time constraints didn't permit us to see a construction site in action; however, we were given a tour of their headquarters and an overview of their program. Since setting up shop in 2001, they've been trying to alleviate the severe housing crisis where, as a result of tradition and economic necessity, extended families live together with up to fifteen people occupying a small two-room building. Kitchens with dirt floors and unsanitary toilet facilities contribute to the unhealthy living conditions. As the vast majority of Jordanians live on less than 3,500 JD (Jordanian dinars) a year (approximately 5,000 U.S. dollars), moving into a habitable home isn't a viable option.

Presently they have builds going on in four rural villages as well as in urban Amman. Groups of overseas volunteers, local schools, and corporate groups help build cement block houses, with the receiving families contributing 1,275 JD (approximately 1,800 U.S. dollars) in the form of labor and donated materials. A family needs to provide the plot of land that they own. Regrettably, Habitat cannot assist the growing flock of refugees crossing the border from Iraq because refugees cannot own land.

On the U.S.-based Habitat builds I've participated in, the God-talk tends to be low-key, with the emphasis on letting Jesus shine through our labors. The only time I ever saw Scriptures on-site was during the dedications, when the new homeowners are given a Holy

Bible (or a Qur'an if the home is for a Muslim family). Such dedications do not take place in Jordan out of respect for religious sensitivities. Still, each new home stands as a silent witness to the fact that God's people are at work rebuilding in the Middle East.

Later I stopped by Amman's only Christian (read: evangelical) bookstore. Except for some Christian kitsch in the children's section, the store looked like a typical upscale café/bookstore. The Jordanian travel books and secular stuff sat up front, while the faith fare took up the back half of the room. From what I gathered, the bulk of their customers come in for coffee and something of a non-religious nature.

Walking through the streets of Amman by myself, I began to see Paul's letter to the Ephesians in a new light. As someone who has been told by Bible Belters that I'm going to burn, baby, burn for all of eternity, I'm well aware of how the fundamentalist faithful take Paul literally at his word when it comes to the proper attire that should be worn by a godly woman — not to mention all this shut-the-heck-up-in-church biz. But I interpret Paul as encouraging his followers to be sensitive to the pervasive culture so that their actions don't cause alienation and division. The people I met treated me with respect because I chose to don a long skirt and a head scarf. Had I worn my blonde hair loose and donned a tank top and shorts, my reception would not have been nearly as gracious.

I had been in Jordan for less than a day, but already the slower pace of this trip, coupled with the melodic chants of the minaret, had started to settle into my bones. I felt my body sinking back into Irish time, where I was guided not by the clock but by the rhythms of the earth.

Unfortunately, I got so absorbed in watching the sun set over Amman that I forgot I had to be back at my hotel before the sun actually set. Then the streets would be deserted once everyone went home to break the fast with their families. After fifteen minutes of slight panic trying to find a cab, several Jordanian teens helped me find a cabdriver who could take me back to the hotel. I tried to tip them for their services, but they refused. I could tell by their appearance that these boys could have used a few dinars.

"No, we just like Americans."

"I like you too. Thank you for your kindness."

On the way back to the hotel, the cabdriver kept telling me how much he liked America. He didn't know enough English for us to engage in a more in-depth conversation. Even if we both knew each other's respective languages, I doubt any Muslim man would divulge personal information with any woman he just met. I did get the sense, though, that these friendly comments weren't simply platitudes they uttered in the hopes of impressing a group of American journalists.

I arrived just as the buffet opened up. Most of our meals were served buffet style, and I made a point of sampling a bit of everything. With the notable exception of lamb brains soaked in yogurt (it tasted as bad as it sounds), the food was delicious; and I developed an addiction to fresh hummus, homegrown olives, and shawarmas.

Holy History!

The next morning, we were driven to Citadel Hill, the embankment where King David royally screwed Uriah (2 Samuel 11:1 – 26). We passed through the temple of Hercules, a thirty-three-foot series of columns built during the reign of the emperor Marcus Aurelius (161 – 180 CE). This archaeological dig remains a work in progress due to lack of funds. Many Jordanian sites are often just "there," with few, if any, identifying historical markers or touristy signs reminding visitors to leave one's guns, dogs, and shorts at home. In contrast to the throngs of merchants who accosted me in Israel, only two men stood inside a tent filled with crafts for sale.

Pat, a fellow journalist with a unique funny bone of her own, and I burst out laughing while touring the Jordan Archaeological Museum. It just seemed too silly to see ancient artifacts housed in what looked like high school trophy cases. In particular, I couldn't believe their collection of bronze Dead Sea Scrolls was shunted off to a corner after I had seen such an ornate display of these priceless artifacts when I was in Israel. Such is the dilemma of a country rich in history but poor in capital.

I see Dead Sea Scrolls.

As our driver escorted us around the city, the seven hills (jabals) of Amman melded together into a mixture of ancient and modern architecture. Honking cars intermingled with the call to prayer. Despite the desert heat, observant Muslims don't drink or eat until sundown during Ramadan. (Except for one accidental slipup, I was able to refrain from eating or drinking on the public streets.)

When we went to visit the King Abdullah Mosque, the women had to wear polyester black-hooded sheaths provided to all female visitors. I tried to focus on our guide's guided prayer session and enjoy the beauty of this Ottoman-style mosque built in 1924, but within minutes, I felt a trickle of sweat down my back. Then another trickle. And another. Drip, drip, drip. Cry me a river — I'm getting drenched. There was no way I could "adjust" myself in a mosque without disgracing our kind guide and the other Muslim men around. Just as I started to sway, our time was up. Out of the spiritual sauna and onward.

The spirit of Ramadan infused me as though I was on a retreat of sorts. I got the impression that a coed group of American tourists who didn't know the Islamic rituals wouldn't be a welcome sight in a mosque, especially during this holy month. (Then again, I've seen plenty of Christians give a visitor the evil eye because this poor soul dared to enter their sacred space without first memorizing that particular church's rules of order.) Although we never performed Salat (prayers) five times a day (well, four actually because I slept through the predawn chants), the haunting adhan (call to prayer) added a balanced rhythm to this trip. My days traveling in and around Amman began to blur as talks about the need for a present-day peace intermingled with seeing ancient history up close and personal.

Our host had the wisdom not to overload our schedule. Unlike Israel, where I traipsed through the Holy Land at a breakneck pace, I could really soak in the pilgrim spirit of this desert. I had some time to see, smell, and touch this sacred soil. During the infrequent windstorms, I even got to taste the sand.

I was in hog heaven when I walked around Gadara (modern-day Umm Qais). The remains of a fourth-century basilica over a tomb indicated the spot where some faithful believe Jesus cast the demons out of two tortured souls and into a herd of swine (Matthew 8:28–34). (I learned from my trek to Israel that others think this miracle occurred at Kursi instead, as both cities are located in the "country of the Gadarenes [or Gerasenes]".)

Taste and see that the LORD is good.
Psalm 34:8

Judging from the distance from Umm Qais to the water, methinks if the miracle occurred at this spot, then at least some of the pigs died from heat exhaustion before they made it to the Sea of Galilee. You'd have to be a seasoned athlete to run a few miles over this hot, rocky desert terrain. With its soft rolling hills, Kursi would have made for an easier jaunt, though once again, I prefer to focus on the healing power of Christ than get all pig-picky here.

At first I didn't get what we were doing in Jerash, but the souvenir salesmen, programmed Arab entertainers, and larger-than-life photo of King Abdullah II told me I must be somewhere "important." Jerash, an amazingly large and well-preserved site of Roman architecture, with ruins going back to the Neolithic age, is also located in the "country of the Gerasenes." Our guide showed us church after church after church with remarkably preserved mosaic tiles built after Constantine converted to Christianity. After a flurry of church-building projects that would put any megachurch pastor to shame, the building stopped pronto. Blame the Persian invasion of 614 CE and then the Muslim conquest of 636.

During our stay in Amman, we were granted meetings with several high-ranking official representatives of the Hashemite Kingdom of Jordan. Unlike pseudo-diplomats such as Jesse Jackson, Angelina Jolie, or George Clooney, I'm just here to listen and learn.

One of the officials we met described how he carried his bleeding comrade out of the hotel after the 11/9 bombing by terrorists in Amman. On November 9, 2005, three suicide bombers with supposed ties to Al Qaeda detonated bombs within minutes of each other at three of Amman's major hotels. These blasts, which killed at least fifty-seven people and injured nearly a hundred, illustrated how we all suffer at the hands of terrorists, whether the Army of God or Al Qaeda. I gathered from their presentations that they wanted to encourage American-Jordanian dialogue. Yes, they regretted the terrorists' actions on our 9/11, though I sensed they get frustrated at times with how American diplomacy gets enacted following that fateful day.

On our last night in Amman, we dined with some Protestant leaders. In our conversation, two items stood out. First, no faith-based entity has the resources to address the ongoing influx of Iraqi refugees. This problem has reached a crisis point that could cripple this country economically. Second, American missionaries who come to "convert" Jordanians end up creating more problems for the miniscule group of Protestants working in this area. (When Baptists based in Jordan tell me to back off on the Bible-thumping, I sit up and listen.)

As one small step forward, perhaps we should lay off using isolated verses from the Qur'an to ascribe pejorative terms to a religion that, like Christianity, sprang forth from Abraham's loins. After all, anyone can mangle sacred texts, New Atheist style, by plucking a particular odious verse from any sacred book and reciting it as though that one line represents the totality of the faith.

For example, here are three bits — one from Hebrew Scripture, one from the New Testament, and one from the Qur'an — that I suspect moderates within each faith might find disheartening:

- "I will make your oppressors eat their own flesh; they will be drunk on their own blood, as with wine" (Isaiah 49:26).
- "Do not suppose that I have come to bring peace to the earth. I did not come to bring peace, but a sword" (Matthew 10:34).
- "I will throw terror into the hearts of those who disbelieved. You may strike them above the necks, and you may strike even every finger" (Sura 8:12).

Here I confess that most of my knowledge comes from reading about Middle Eastern culture rather than exploring how others live out their sacred texts. (Heck, I can get quite confused trying to figure out how American Christians can come to such diverse interpretations of select New Testament passages.) Time for me to open up my ears and hopefully my heart.

Actions really do speak — and witness — louder than words. Perhaps the most often paraphrased advice from St. Francis is that we are to preach the gospel and, if necessary, use words.

Tony Campolo, *The God of Intimacy and Action*

From on top of Mount Nebo, we got a Moses'-eye view of the Promised Land. Unfortunately, the haze prevented us from seeing all the way to Jerusalem. But we could stand on the platform built when Pope John Paul II came to Jordan to mark the Great Jubilee of the Year 2000. A stone memorial commemorated the spot where Moses was alleged to have been buried by God himself, though the location of his actual tomb remains unknown. No sign of the tabernacle and the ark of the covenant that Jeremiah supposedly hid (2 Maccabees 2:4–5).

As I stepped inside the fourth-century church built on the top of Mount Nebo, a quiet calm took me by surprise. I had been so accus-

Stairway to Heaven

tomed to being poked and prodded every time I entered a sanctuary in Israel that I couldn't believe I could actually set foot inside a Holy Land sacred site and simply "be." As our guide began explaining the history of the well-preserved Byzantine mosaics, I chose to tune out. Somehow I felt that whatever it was I needed to learn at this moment could be discerned by my other senses. In all honesty, I didn't have a religious revelation, an intellectual insight, or even a mountaintop moment. I just reveled in the silence and stillness.

At that moment, I started to get a sense of the pilgrim pull that draws disciples to these desert hills. I could have stayed and meditated on Mount Nebo, though the lack of any food or water would have sent me down the mountain after a few hours. (How Jesus fasted for forty days in this desert climate remains a mystery to me [Matthew 4: 1–11]. This helps explain why some of the desert fathers went off the devotional deep end. I'd be delusional too if I stayed in this desert heat for more than a few days.)

As the trip progressed, about a third of us developed some form of a stomach bug. During our brief trek through bits of Wadi Rum, we pulled up to a Bedouin camp for a buffet that I wish I could have enjoyed. Although the bumpy Jeep ride nearly caused my cup to runneth over, I soaked in the romance of Lawrence of Arabia before we headed on to the seaside town of Aqaba.

Historical Happenings

Despite its history as a major port and a hub for those trading in Asia, Africa, and Europe, Aqaba gets only a few mentions in the Bible. Here King Solomon set up a shipbuilding business (1 Kings 9:26) and the queen of Sheba came for a visit (1 Kings 10:1–13). So when our guide pointed to the remains of a church next to a parking lot, I wondered what would prompt a small band of Christians to set up shop in Aqaba. Maybe they came here for the commerce and then became Christians.

Frankly, there wasn't much to see, as this was yet another dig in progress. We're talking a teeny-weeny chapel about 85 feet by 52 feet, a far cry from a majestic structure like the Church of the Nativity in Bethlehem that was built about a hundred years later. There wasn't even a fence to keep the animals and curious onlookers at bay. In fact, if I hadn't read the smudged letters on the faded blue sign, I'd have no clue I was standing in front of a piece of church history being unwrapped before me like some early Christmas present — a bit of Holy Land history that's just being reborn.

These religious remains date back to around 290 CE. We're talking pre–Edict of Milan, before Constantine created his empire-evangelization campaign. Hence, Christianity remained an illegal activity in which followers of Jesus conducted their services in house churches away from the gaze of the Roman guards. What, then, would prompt a group of persecuted people to build a church in plain sight? How come the Romans let this structure stand? All that greeted me was stony silence.

But the more than two million pieces of colored stone comprising the Madaba Mosaic Map still speak to pilgrims. This sixth-century map, which covers portions of the floor of the Greek Orthodox Church of St. George in Madaba, told the story of the physical layout of Jerusalem after its destruction and rebuilding in 70 CE. Even though this church was built in 1896 over the remains of an earlier sixth-century Byzantine church, this site retains a very ancient air.

I could have meditated for hours at this map, retracing my steps throughout Israel and Jordan. And I wish we would have hiked up Mukawir, the mountain where supposedly John the Baptist lost his head (Matthew 14:3–12; Mark 6:17–29). As enticing as these options might have been, Petra called. I didn't want to miss out on participating in my own Hollywood-style action adventure.

God-Smacked Again

I woke up more excited than an Apocalypse addict all dressed up in angel white, waiting to be raptured. Since I'm an outdoor enthusiast, getting to play in one of the New Seven Wonders of the World sits right at the top of my bucket list. Petra ("stone" in Greek) stands in the land referenced as Edom in the Old Testament and gets mentioned in the Bible under names such as Sela and Joktheel (2 Kings 14:7). So we had somewhat of a biblical basis for spending an entire day playing in Petra.

Although the ruins of a nine-thousand-year-old city north of Petra called Beidha indicate this land has prehistoric roots, nothing is recorded about this area until the Edomites come onto the scene during the Iron Age (circa 1200 BCE). After King David "struck them down" (biblical code for "ethnic cleansing"; 1 Chronicles 18:11 – 13), the Edomites faced an ongoing series of attacks from the Judeans. Then the nomadic Nabateans took over in the sixth century BCE when they entered this valley. The city's good fortune as a trading hub enabled the inhabitants to carve the temples, tombs, sculptures, and other buildings into the rocks. With all this commercial traffic, one could conclude that the three kings stopped by Petra en route to Bethlehem (Matthew 2:1 – 12).

As expected, the Romans weren't too pleased with this empire in progress. They launched a series of attacks and conquered the Nabatean Kingdom in 106 CE and Romanized the joint. By the time of the Muslim conquest in the seventh century CE, Petra had fallen into obscurity. After a brief renaissance during the Crusades, the city seemed to vanish into thin air until Johann Ludwig Burckhardt rediscovered Petra in 1812.

But enough history. I wanted to play.

When we came upon the Indiana Jones gift and snack shops, I got the giggles. I had been so immersed in experiencing these

holy sites without being accosted by merchants that I completely forgot that some folks might want to make a buck out of Jordan's number one tourist attraction. Except for the name, there was nothing really adventurous about either sidewalk shop. The snack shop looked like some rundown deli that someone plastered a metal sign on the front of in the hopes the name might bring in some business. While the gift shop had a slightly more elaborate-looking sign, replete with a drawing of Harrison Ford, the interior shrieked "tacky, tacky, tacky."

The Titanic Coffee Shop sits to the side. However, calling this pink hut surrounded by soda machines a "coffee shop" might be somewhat of a stretch. Frankly, I have no clue what connection there might be between a holy site carved in stone and the infamous ship that sank. Tempted as I was to go into the Titanic and order an iced coffee, I suspected my humor might not translate.

A slew of guides accosted us at the entrance to see if we wanted to be walked in on a horse. After we politely declined their offers, our group trotted off on a sandy path. Soon we passed what would be the first of many tombs to come.

After we turned the corner, I felt Lilliputian standing below a row of 400- to 650-foot ragged sandstone mountains. We walked between two massive rocks via the Siq, a narrow gorge filled with natural ravines and fissures. Everywhere I turned along this approximately half-mile path, Mother Nature or an earthborn artisan had carved a sculpture, water channel, shrine to some deity, or some other design into the stone.

Out of the corner of my eye I caught a peek of al-Khazneh (the Treasury). With each step, the Treasury came closer and closer until

finally I stood in front of this royal tomb carved into the rock. Built sometime between 100 BCE and 200 CE, the tomb got its name from the legend that pirates hid their treasure in a giant stone urn. Bullet holes on the urn indicate that the Bedouins believed this myth and made numerous attempts to retrieve this booty.

At that point, I was on such sensory overload that I couldn't comprehend any more history. I stared up at this edifice, wondering how skilled workers managed to climb about 140 feet to create such magical perfection that I thought I was on a movie set. After pinching myself a few times, I brought myself back to reality and hustled to rejoin the group.

We approached an eight-thousand-seat Roman amphitheater surrounded by a burial bonanza. Local Bedouins used to occupy the caves we spotted off in the distance. The government outlawed this practice in 1984 out of a concern to preserve the monuments. The Bedouins resettled nearby, though as a compromise of sorts, they're the only merchants allowed to conduct commerce inside the walls of Petra.

Fortunately, tents displaying their wares were kept to a minimum. According to our guide, when traveling in Jordan, you should look for items with the Noor Al-Hussein Foundation seal of approval (though the sign may read Queen Noor Foundation, as it did in Petra). This tells you that your gift is helping artisans achieve economic independence and take care of their families.

After lunch, Pat and I chose to ride up to al-Deir (the Monastery) on donkeys. The thought of climbing up eight hundred steep steps as the temperature hovered near 100 degrees didn't sound appealing. Horses and camels balk at this almost vertical climb, but

donkeys can do it. We were told to just hold on to the horn and the donkey would keep us in our saddle.

The donkeys clomped along a relatively flat surface. No problemo. Then the path narrowed and steepened, and we passed over patches of cobble crumbs. My stomach felt a bit like it did the first time I rode the Coney Island Cyclone. Still, my donkey never missed a step, stopping only to relieve himself. (My sympathy for those who chose to walk to the monastery, because the path was littered with donkey dung.)

Once our donkeys crossed over the final step, we dismounted and walked up a small hill toward this craggy, unfinished edifice.

The crosses inside the walls indicate that the monastery might have been used as a church or a hermitage, though historians think it was probably a temple.

When we stopped for a bit of water, a vendor suggested that we might want to visit a nearby scenic overlook. I wasn't sure my heart could absorb any more beauty, but I decided to run with the local recommendation.

Slowly I walked up the short dusty path. Since there were no guardrails at the mountain's edge, I carefully approached the crest. With each step, purple peaks winked at me as though daring me

---

The Four Best Moments for Donkeys
as reported by Jason Boyett in *The Pocket Guide to the Bible*

Balaam's donkey speaks (Numbers 22:23 – 30). In one of the most original biblical miracles ever, Balaam's donkey is given the gift of speech when his master encounters an angel of the Lord on the path. Even weirder, Balaam jumps right in and engages the suddenly literate beast of burden in conversation, without so much as batting an eyelash.

Samson kills a thousand Philistines with the "jawbone of a donkey" (Judges 15:13 – 17). And while today, Jackie Chan types can turn pool cues and potted plants into deadly armaments, the donkey-bone-as-weapon trend never really catches on.

Donkeys are praised for their large genitals (Ezekiel 23:20). No, really. And by none other than God himself, in a sexually explicit metaphor condemning Israel's unfaithfulness.

Jesus makes his triumphal entry on the back of a donkey (Mark 11:1 – 11). Which cements the humble donkey as one of the earth's holiest creatures. Or, perhaps, not.

(I'd add a fifth moment to this list. While the New Testament doesn't indicate the mode of transportation Joseph and Mary employed to get to Bethlehem, almost every artistic rendering of the birth narratives has Jesus making his humble entry into the world thanks to a diligent donkey [Matthew 1 – 2; Luke 1 – 2].)

to venture into God's playpen, a spectacle of nature so vast that the Grand Canyon seems like a watering hole in comparison. As stunning as the man-made Treasury and Monastery might be (and they are truly magnificent wonders of the world), nothing can surpass the beauty of God's own artistic endeavors.

When it was time to return, we saw our donkeys waiting patiently for us. As challenging as going up eight hundred steps might have been, heading down proved to be even worse. It was like riding a roller coaster in reverse. Almost every time my donkey took a step, I felt my body tilting out of the saddle. But my donkey never flinched. Nothing deterred him from his destination. No wonder a donkey carried Jesus to his birth and death. Clearly, this is the only animal with the stamina to get the job done every time. One might be mocked for riding an ass instead of a royal Arabian horse or a kingly camel — but Jesus was noted for turning the world upside down.

When Jesus rode into Jerusalem on a donkey, his followers brandishing palm branches, this satirical street theatre represented a form of political protest guaranteed to tick off the Romans. The crowd had witnessed enough Roman pageantry to know full well the symbolism behind these joking gestures. Such moves come with a price — mock the Roman imperial procession and the next thing you know, you're carrying your cross.

> *We can never forget that we're just the asses who've been corralled to help bring Jesus in.*
> **Shane Claiborne**

Thankfully, the story didn't end at Calvary. The Holy Land still speaks today. Just listen to the donkeys.

After I scrubbed the donkey smell from my skin and had dinner, we set out for Petra by night. A group of too-talkative tourists killed the mystical mood for a bit, but eventually we maneuvered our way around the crowd and found a quieter place to pray as we walked along the candlelit path.

After entering the Treasury, we watched an Arabian Nights performance. I chose not to join the sit-down crowd because I had a major case of donkey butt. Assuming Mary rode a donkey, did her heinie hurt this much by the time she made it into Bethlehem? (A rough rear end represented the least of Jesus' Passover problems.)

After such a holy high, the next day we got down and dirty by driving around Sodom and Gomorrah. Obviously there's nothing left after God did a fire-and-brimstone dance all over these "wicked" cities. I didn't spot any salt statues — perhaps the local donkeys in ages past had discovered an extra-large salt lick — though we were taken to Lot's cave near the town of Zoar (now called Safi). Yep, this marked the infamous spot where Lot's daughters started singing "dirty daddy deeds done dirt cheap" and gave birth to sons who would become the Ammonites and Moabites. Judging by this tiny hut, Lot wasn't living large, that's for sure (Genesis 19).

Lord of the Faith Flies

After leaving Lotland, we set out for Bethany Beyond the Jordan. Based on my experiences in seeing the Israeli side of the Jordan, I knew not to expect a majestic, flowing river. Still, we were about to hit the very spot where, according to Christian tradition, the religious rubber hit the road, courtesy of John's Bethany baptisms.

I was baptized by my father, the Rev. Karl Claudius Garrison Jr., when I was six weeks old. So I have no actual recollection of the moment when the waters of baptism marked me as one of Christ's own forever. Still, I felt a primal pull to visit this low-lying desert region where supposedly Jesus was baptized, the heavens opened up, and God gave his Son a high five (Matthew 3:13–17; Mark 1:9–11; Luke 3:21–22; John 1:29–34).

Throughout history, scholars debated ad infinitum the exact moment when Jesus knew he was to be the Messiah. Still, after John gave Jesus a divine dunking and a voice from the heavens boomed out, "This is my son, whom I love; with him I am well pleased" (Matthew 3:17), didn't that pretty much seal the deal?

When I trekked down to the Jordan River, the earthiness of the Holy Land hit me squarely in the face. The temperature was pushing 100 degrees Fahrenheit, and the stagnant water made it a bit hard to breathe. At least the calm air kept the desert sand from swirling all around me.

Why in God's name would John have chosen this dusty dump as the focal point of his ministry? I guess this is what you'd expect from a man who draped himself in camel-hair clothing and ate locusts and honey (Mark 1:6). Lovely.

I walked along the Israeli side of the Jordan River without any guards, but in Jordan I had to cross through several checkpoints manned by soldiers. I pondered how the Roman guards might have interacted with John and his disciples. By now I've been to a host of Holy Land sites. Yet I always get very uneasy when I see guns guarding the very sites where God intervened in human history.

I passed the ruins of ancient churches scattered around the site. Clearly I wasn't the only pilgrim searching for a personal connection to the divine. I wanted to stop and pray for a bit, but every time I tried to stand still, a plethora of flies showered me with their blessings. They reminded me of those too-friendly church ushers who greet me with such godly gusto that I get the spiritual heebie-jeebies. Now I get the irony of the Israelites mocking the Canaanite ruler by calling him Beelzebub, a.k.a. Lord of the Flies. Funny! (Don't worry, I didn't grab the conch or organize any pig-hunting parties.)

Despite these awful conditions, when I touched the water, I felt a peace pass over me. This doubting Thomas had to touch the river in order to understand why John stopped here, but as soon as I did, I knew it in my bones: From the lowest point on earth, the heavens opened up and God anointed the King of kings. Thus marked the start of this topsy-turvy kingdom that turned the entire world upside down.

I tried to sit still and meditate, but the flies had a particular penchant for wet skin. They hovered around me until I slapped myself silly. My precious peace was further broken by an older couple from New Jersey who came to the river with gallon jugs in tow. For a moment, I wish I had saved my water bottles so I could preserve this moment; but you can't capture this kind of a sensory sensation.

When I got up to leave, our guide informed us that the land right next to us was Israel. This neighboring Holy Land was only a hop, skip, and jump away from us. However, with a guard watching us in the distance and armed with an assault rifle, I didn't dare slosh across to the other side.

By now, the hellish heat had me longing for those ubiquitous tourist shops on the Israeli side of the Jordan River where one could purchase bottled water. But we were about to get refreshed beyond our wildest dreams.

Life saver at the Jordan River

Our host provided us with a day-and-a-half stay at a five-star luxury hotel on the Dead Sea. I soaked in the mud, floated in the sea, and chilled in the spa's whirlpools until I was a puddle of glop. The last time I felt this gooey was back in Glendalough when I let God rain all over me. Once again, God chose to communicate to me through his creation, not to mention my own mini-Balaamlike revelation at Petra.

Except for chatting with some officials and church leaders, I didn't really interact much with many Jordanians. Yes, we don't speak the same language, though perhaps our hearts connected on some level by sharing the same soil.

On my last night in Jordan, speckles of light emanated from Jerusalem as though God winked at me. I gazed over at Israel, raised my glass, and offered a toast to the heavens.

A Divine Nobody
Meets the Wright Stuff

OCTOBER 2007

E ver since I took my first ride on the information superhighway back in 1995, I've been a bit hesitant about the whole nature of cyberchurch. If Jesus came back today, I wonder how the Internet would influence his ministry.

> *Our identity as a collective body is being recontextualized from a local level to a simultaneous embrace of both local and global relationships — what Roland Robertson [chair in sociology and global society, University of Aberdeen] calls "glocal" awareness.*
>
> **John La Grou,** *Voices of the Virtual World*

How would Jesus react to seeing his followers worshiping together in cyberspace without ever meeting face-to-face? Which social networking sites, if any, would his disciples employ to show others "The Way"? How would Jesus deal with the anonymity of the Internet, where a reasonable religious discussion can digress into a biblical brawl and spread like a plague of locusts? I know I've had my share of online arguments that could have been avoided had we met in person for a few beers.

No matter how wired Christians might be, I sense our Lord and Savior would insist that we sit down every so often for some real face time. I communicated with my Greenbelt contacts for years,

GENTLEMEN, I BELIEVE THERE IS
AN IMPOSTOR IN OUR CONVERSATION

but we didn't really connect as brothers and sisters in Christ until we hugged each other face-to-face.

So when I was invited to lead a few workshops during Soularize 2007, I welcomed the chance to actually meet some of the people who were reading my articles.

"What the heck. Sign me up. Sounds like fun."

Any group that can bring together keynote speakers like N. T. Wright, Rita Brock, Richard Rohr, and Brennan Manning has got to be more than a bit theologically twisted. Add into the mix some formerly fried church planters, a bunch of bloggers, a few eager postevangelicals, some California creatives, and a group of folks waiting to join the party from around the world thanks to the magic of the Internet, and you've got all the makings for a red-hot learning party.

I arrived a day late to the fun due to flight delays. (On the plus side, a friend from divinity school lives in Miami, and we had a quick unexpected visit when I found myself stranded stateside.) Once I finally landed in the Bahamas and checked into my hotel,

I found out no one left any information for me at the front desk. Rather than go off on some righteous rant, I decided to strike a Bahamian pose. I hit the beach and the Jacuzzi, praying that, as at Greenbelt, everything would work out amid all this chaos.

By chance, I ran into someone in the elevator who was leaving in fifteen minutes to go to some church. Turns out our sessions would be held indoors instead of on the beach or poolside. Oh, and the shuttles weren't free. Once I factored in this additional expense, this event ceased being a cost-effective Christian conference. I found myself shelling out significant bucks for what I thought would be a learning vacation held poolside at a swanky resort. Instead, I was going to be inside a church most of the time. Also, most of the male leaders chose to stay at an all-boys condo instead of having us all chill together at the same hotel. This wasn't the big inclusive party I'd hoped for — it was like high school all over again, and I'm the unpopular weirdo writer.

Granted, there were a few more Christian chicks here than at other evangelical and emergent gatherings I've attended, but it was still at least 85 percent white males. From what I could see from the table configurations, most of them preferred to keep it that way.

Now, if one comes from a conservative tradition in which women get relegated to running children's church and organizing potluck suppers, the thought of "allowing" women to be part of the big boys' discussion must be liberating. But I come from a tradition that has legally ordained women since 1979 and currently has a woman wearing the biggest pointy hat. A host of other folks have become accustomed to worshiping in environments where

Where da white women at?
Bart (Cleavon Little), *Blazing Saddles*

women do a heckuva lot more than man the nursery. This endless talk about the need to be more inclusive puts me to sleep when the end results tend to be still pretty much the same old song.

The moment the music started and I saw some hands reach up for the sky, I headed for the door. Back in the 1980s, I'd be waving and swaying like we were all channeling the identical theological tune. But these days I bolt whenever I hear "Jesus is my boyfriend" music. Thinking about Jesus caressing me and then getting all inside of me makes me want to take a cold spiritual shower.

However, the lack of transportation options meant I had no choice but to stop and listen. So I sat there kind of grumpy. After the third song, I started to mellow. Dang it. Worship leader Barry Taylor is good. I mean really good. His original creations possess more substance than what I tend to dismiss as crummy Christian music.

After Barry finished playing, I got to hear N. T. Wright. While I had interviewed the good bishop for *The Wittenburg Door*, Soularize marked the first time I could spend some time really observing how this Anglican heavyweight interacted with a largely evangelical audience.

Wright served up some theological tidbits from his forthcoming book *Surprised by Hope*. In a nutshell, he refuted the prevailing rapture-ready eschatology that the elect will be ushered into a "new heaven and new earth" while we heathens will be left behind

in the hopes that the Rayford Steele character (or another one of Jerry Jenkins's creations) will save us. Also, he debunked the traditional notion that "heaven" refers to some ethereal fluffy and flowery place where after death, we get cast in a Hollywood remake of *Heaven Can Wait.*

At this point, I thought the bulk of this Christian crowd would bolt. But then I remembered I'm in the land of Ooze. Like Dorothy, I'm not in Christian Kansas anymore. Now, I wouldn't call the mostly male crowd gathered here missional monkeys or munchkins. But Spencer Burke, the learning party planner, could be the cowardly lion, though he's more hyper-friendly, like Toto. Richard Rohr's got some tin man in him, and Brennan Manning's patchwork pants give him a scarecrow look. I'm not sure if Rita Brock would want to be thought of as Gilda the Good Witch, though she did present a positive view of a progressive paradise.

N. T. Wright could be cast as the Wizard of Oz, though he's no magician taking us to some imaginary la-la land. Some academics seem to enjoy partaking in post-Christian kamikaze runs, dropping cluster bombs of theological TNT on unsuspecting church folks without placing their pomo ponderings into their proper sociopolitical and historical contexts.

Fortunately, Wright pilots the plane down to earth. He puts on his bishop's mitre to offer practical and pastoral counsel regarding how the "church" as defined as "the body of the faithful" becomes the vessel through which this kingdom becomes manifest into this world.

Throughout his talks, one could hear the tap-tap-tap sound of bloggers firing away on all pistons. I preferred to sit and soak it all in. Like good single malt, Wright needs to be savored and sipped.

That's not to say I was calm, cool, and collected. Technical and scheduling difficulties proved to be monster headaches that prevented my online workshop from getting off the ground, while my in-person workshop wasn't taped properly. I attended specifically so I would be in a post-Soularize boxed product because I wanted to prove that chicks have a place at the table. But it looked like I was out of the box in more ways than one.

In my frustrated and confused state, I really didn't hear Brennan Manning's talks. But when I finally picked up his books *Abba's Child* and *The Furious Longing of God*, I felt an immediate bond with this man who is just as messy as I am. We're both kind of raggedy in our own ways.

Brennan's books are not for the fainthearted searching for a quick spiritual fix. This Franciscan priest ended up on the streets with nothing to his name. Instead of wallowing in the pains and problems of his life, Brennan talks about how God's love saved him — literally. This "love" wasn't mere fuzzy sentimentality but rather an expression of God's deep desire to love all of us. This ferocious love includes a longing to touch those dark parts of ourselves we keep hidden from the world.

His stark honesty as he bore his scar tissue of his life caught me off my guard. I wasn't expecting a book to connect with me on such a visceral level. Through Brennan's story, I saw how I had veered way off the path. For all of my talk about how we need to put the Greatest Commandment into practice, I wasn't exactly practicing what I preached. Too often, I focused so much on trying to "do good" and "help people" that I had failed to love them just as they are. When several people let me down, my anger got the better of me, and some things came out of my mouth and pen that were more critical than Christlike.

The kernel that I picked up from Brennan's books is that while God longs to connect with me, in order for me to connect with God, I must first connect with others in love. He reminds us:

> The outstretched arms of Jesus exclude no one, not the drunk in the doorway, the panhandler on the street, gays and lesbians in their isolation, the most selfish and ungrateful in their cocoons, the most unjust of employers and the most overweening of snobs. The love of Christ embraces all without exception.

I wish I wouldn't keep forgetting this core message of the gospel. But I do.

Fortunately, I was alert enough to connect with fellow author Jim Palmer. We both grew up in homes where we were deemed worthless garbage. After his marriage fell apart, he left the church he founded and started frequenting local hangouts like Waffle House. In this process of listening to waitresses, truck drivers, neighbors, and other people who operate below the religious radar, he learned that God loved him with no strings attached. Rather than carve out a platform for him to sell his pastoral product, Jim embraced the idea of becoming "a divine nobody." Like all those people he meets, he doesn't hold any official position of power in the religious world. He just "is."

In my rantings against select elite emergent/progressive church circles, I flung more than my share of holy crap. Perhaps rather than continuing to engage in theological turf wars that only serve to bloody the body of Christ, I should embrace this whole "divine nobody" biz.

Easier said than done. Right now, I'm still fuming over how my planned vacation got religiously rear-ended.

After Soularize, I got to participate in a two-day workshop led by Richard Rohr on Christian spirituality and enneagrams. Back in the early 1990s, I took a Myers-Briggs test. (I'm ENTJ, for those of you who are into this stuff.) These results led to a major aha moment. Now I could see why certain folks made me crazy. We're wired differently. When our wiring crossed, we ended up shocking each other.

Now I got a chance to apply this type of analysis to my spiritual life. I learned I'm an eight. We're the mavericks, the visionaries who buck hierarchy and prefer to work solo. (I knew I hated being a "team player," and now I know why.) We're also the ones who say what has to be said without giving a rip who we offend. Hence, we often find ourselves standing alone in a field because no one wants to be near us for fear we might shoot their sacred cow. (Yep, that pretty much fits the job description of a religious satirist.) When we're fully grounded in the gospel, we can move mountains, like Martin Luther King Jr. did. At our worst, we resemble our fellow eights Saddam Hussein, Fidel Castro, and Al Capone.

Our prickly personalities make it difficult for us to form emotional attachments. But when we bond, we're like spiritual superglue. That explains why I go absolutely ballistic when a "friend" betrays me. If we're not careful, our anger can get the best of us. That's been my story more times than I care to admit. Sometimes as a satirist, I keep hammering on the king after he's been dethroned. Then instead of hunting down sacred cows, I end up shooting puppies. Kicking a religious rocker after he's sung his last unholy song and hit the spiritual skids is cruel, not cool.

This post-Soularize retreat, coupled with the Wright stuff, gave this newly self-described "divine nobody" more than ample faith food to digest. But just as we were packing for the airport, we got word that Tropical Storm Noel was headed toward the Bahamas and we had to evacuate immediately. Guess I wouldn't be taking that one last contemplative walk on the beach after all.

My plane took off for Miami right before they shut down the airport. The tropical rain pelted the plane like a woodpecker on crack, thus rendering me unable to read or relax. What a way to end one weird weekend.

Once my head and the weather cleared, I began to see how connections happened despite myself. Out of this unfortunate chaos came some semblance of community. I found a number of folks I still communicate with via email and Facebook. These divine nobodies remind me that I need to shift my focus away from those who keep trying to manufacture some theological tsunami that will usher in yet another unmissional revolution. What if we turned instead to see where the Holy Spirit might be taking us, hurricanes and all? Can I trust that just as Jesus saved Peter, he'll rescue me of little faith as well (Matthew 14:22 – 33; Mark 6:45 – 52; John 6:16 – 21)?

Cashing In
at the Christian Casinos

NOVEMBER 2007

When I learned that the 2007 American Academy of Reli-
gion/Society of Biblical Literature (AAR/SBL) meeting
would be held in San Diego, where my brother and his family live,
and that Church Publishing wanted to throw a launch party for
my new book *Rising from the Ashes: Rethinking Church* (and a few
of their other titles), I started packing for California. Despite my
best intentions to transform my trips into pilgrimages, I had serious
doubts I would find one nanosecond of downtime in San Diego
between the book launch, interviews, exhibitors, seminars, parties,
and, of course, familial fun.

The Saturday morning session on Emergent Church jolted me
more than a double shot of fair trade espresso. My late father was
a college professor and an Episcopal priest, so I'm well aware how
academic antics and pastoral pranks can reach biblical proportions
that would put even Cecil B. DeMille to shame. But AAR/SBL
represents a top-notch gathering of international academic elites.
Why, then, was I sitting through what looked like *The Theological
Twilight Zone*?

Setting aside the jokes about cigars and jeans that one tends
to hear more at a fraternity smoker than an academic seminar, all
this talk about "reimagining" the church appeared to be a religious remix of the past. Substitute stools for pulpits, use sofas in
lieu of pews, and say progressive instead of liberal — voila, you've
got a postevangelical church. But all this sounds oddly familiar to

the late-night psychedelic sessions my late father, the Rev. Dr. Karl Claudius Garrison Jr., held with his college students back in the sixties, sans *The White Album* blaring in the background. I was a kid at the time, so I don't recall the specific nuances of these utopian dialogues (though given the haze that permeated the family living room, I wonder what anyone remembers from this era).

Can anyone really blame the current church crises on "bad theology," as though all of Christendom needs a universal spiritual spanking of sorts? Yes, those who believe in black-and-white would benefit from painting with a more multi-hued palate. Hence, I applaud efforts to help fundies stop beating themselves up biblically and find more holistic and healthy ways of interacting with God.

But what about those of us who come from historical traditions with a solid theology? I, for one, am a happy hooker (as in the theologian Richard Hooker, not the madam Xaviera Hollander). In fact, the richness of the Episcopal Church's liturgy has led some postevangelical church plants to adopt portions of *The Book of Common Prayer* in their gatherings.

Simply put, the U.S. Episcopal Church's problem isn't "bad theology" but rather "bad gardening." Unfortunately, it let its treasured traditions rust away in some toolbox. But Greenbelt showed me how some UK Anglicans have started caring for their gardens. Looks to me like their U.S. Episcopal counterparts need some new seeds and a heckuva lot of hard work.

Right about this time, the fly fisher in me kicked in. (Thinking about water always tends to calm me, and, Lord knows, I needed to chill right about then.) This ongoing debate between independent church plants and denominational structures seems to be akin to talking about saltwater versus freshwater fly-fishing. Jesus was a fisher of men after all (John 21:1–13). In both instances, the ultimate objective remains to catch fish. However, the gear and technologies employed to land a forty-inch striped bass would scare the living daylights out of a wily rainbow trout. (Yes, I have caught a sucker that big; and when it comes to fishing, size matters. This particular analogy doesn't apply though to church communities, where bigger often means blander.)

Regardless of the type of fish we're targeting, we'll all probably end up having a great day on the water if we focus on fishing in those places that speak to our hearts. I cast my line in the UK-U.S. Anglican stream, while occasionally dipping my toe into other international waters. Pick the spot that works best for you — just don't pee in my pond. Yes, analogous to their church counterparts, a few male anglers will do anything to keep chicks off the water. Having a guy whack the water with his rod (or worse) really puts the damper on a day of fine fishing or worshiping. Given that I lack the necessary ontological equipment to engage in such manly matters, I tend to walk away from such shooting matches.

I heard similar clarion calls about the potential to create a new inclusive church community when I volunteered at Ground Zero after 9/11, when select individuals tried to take the collective spirit harnessed during the recovery effort and invest it into future ministries. In hindsight, I see how in both those instances, the communal spirit morphed into one-man shows replete with self-appointed experts, conferences, and publishing deals that in both cases appear to have fizzled out, for the most part.

> *I also think we're susceptible to false community because we have a deep-heart knowing of some of how it should be. There must be a seed of the garden of Eden planted in our view of community, and we search for it intuitively. Having so rarely seen or experienced The Real, we fall too easily for The Spiel.*
>
> **Brad Sargent,** futuristguy

I learned in my travels that creating genuine Christian community takes more than degrees, conferences, and theological smackdowns. Andrew Jones offers this sage counsel: "Anarchy and nihilism don't build strong communities, and art must flow from a healed space to be life giving." As much as Christians can benefit from robust critiques of the faith from academic atheists like Freud, Heidegger, and Žižek, I've noticed that Dorothy Day, Dietrich Bonhoeffer, and Jesus of Nazareth tend to end up at the kiddie table whenever these heavy hitters get invited to the banquet as guests of honor.

When I watch some of these guys perform, I feel like I'm listening to a Christian cover band; depending on the group's musical talents, their tunes range from easy on the ears to cat-in-the-dryer quality. But they're all songs and speeches I've heard before. Nothing beats the vibe of authenticity when a musician or a writer speaks from the depth of his or her being.

Blogger Bill Kinnon confesses to "a profound weariness with the kool kids who want to blow up the present church to create what — a groovy new way of doing church? They spend more time dancing with the words of Foucault, whilst wearing Lyotard's, than struggling with St. Paul in 1 Corinthians 13." Paul clearly had a stellar education, as, according to tradition, he was taught by the great rabbi Gamaliel. But post-Damascus, he adapted his message to his audiences so they could hear the gospel in the cultural context that spoke to their hearts (1 Corinthians 9:19 – 23).

A CHURCH OF LOOSE AND OPEN MINDED CHRISTIANS

Despite my growing cynicism, I get the enthusiasm and passion directed toward new movements of the Spirit. I recall my Cursillo days back in the 1980s when I thought I had discovered *the* church. According to its website, Cursillo represents "a movement that, through a method of its own, tries to, and through God's grace manages to, enable the essential realities of the Christian to come to life in the uniqueness, originality, and creativity of each person."

After Cursillo came into my life, I felt like my faith was on fire for the first time. I got so excited about how Cursillo helped me find the "one true faith" that I couldn't wait to share this "good news" with anyone and everyone, regardless of whether they wanted to hear it. All too often, in my zealous state, I acted like an overexcited puppy that licks strangers and then tries to mount them before soiling the carpet.

As an overeager evangelist, I preached what I thought was the way, the truth, and the life. I had all the answers, but no time for questions or even reasoned debate. At times, my critical thinking went out the window, like the zealots who followed Brian instead of Jesus in *Life of Brian*. Regrettably, I dismissed those who walked away when I tried to share the joys of Cursillo as being stick-in-the-mud, misguided messes.

The late Judy Baumer, my first spiritual director, somehow managed not to laugh in my face. In her infinite wisdom, she gently began feeding me a healthy diet of ancient mystics such as St. John of the Cross, Julian of Norwich, and the Desert Fathers, coupled with servings of modern spiritual heavyweights like Basil Pennington, Henri Nouwen, and Gerald May. As I delved into these resources, I felt my faith moving beyond the Cursillo crowd. I can still feel the shunned looks when I told these spiritual stalwarts that I needed to leave this cliquelike Christianity. Still, I remain grateful that Cursillo got me started in my quest to "follow Jesus."

So I fully understand those who discover a movement that finally makes their faith become real and revealed. For I, too, thought I had received a divine revelation from God about what it means to "be the church." Now I see that what I experienced was but a spark of the Holy Spirit. Together, all our sparks join forces to create the fire that fuels our faith (though if we're not careful, we'll set ourselves on fire as if we're at some biblical Burning Man festival). Setting aside the claims of some that they have drafted the ultimate manifesto that will establish the church of the future, history reveals that none of us hold the only match.

> *Rather than a set of directions to get saved, Jesus is, as his earliest followers claimed, "the Way." Jesus is not the way we get somewhere. Jesus is the Christian journey itself, a pilgrimage that culminates in the wayfarer's arrival in God.*
> **Diana Butler Bass,** *Christianity for the Rest of Us*

Through sociologist Diana Butler Bass's astute eyes, I realized how the diverse interfaith encounters I've been having over all these years parallel the experiences she recorded as well. Her penetrating and probing question, "What are we emerging from and where are we emerging to?" provided me with much-needed historical clarity by reminding me that the church has been transforming since the time of the book of Acts.

So that we don't all get seasick during this spiritual sea change, we need to view these current debates through the lens of church history. Terms like *emergent, monasticism,* and *doubt* aren't brand-spanking-new postmodern terms coined toward the end of the twentieth century. Andrew Jones notes that the first instance he found of the use of the word *emergent* was in a document detailing the propositions of the Synod of the churches of New England, which convened in Boston in 1662.

Now, I'm not about to give the institutional church a clean bill of health. But let's put things into their proper historical perspective, shall we? For instance, when debating contemporary church problems such as the U.S. Episcopal crisis over the consecration of homosexual bishops and the blessing of same-sex marriage, calling this faith fight a "schism" brings to mind a Christian catastrophe like the Great Schism of 1064 that separated Roman Catholics from their Eastern Orthodox brethren. In comparison, a group of

100,000 Anglicans defecting from the 80 million–member Anglican Communion resembled a case of the spiritual sniffles. When left unchecked, a malady of this nature can become quite irritating, though not fatal.

If the church was indeed destined for total annihilation, then the walls would have tumbled down some five hundred years ago. Yes, today's church fights can be quite debilitating at times. But methinks if the Internet had been around during the time of the Reformation, the faith fights among the devotees of Cranmer, Calvin, Luther, Knox, and Zwingli would make today's blog battles pale in comparison. Yet the church not only survived; she thrived — albeit in different cultural contexts.

While spiritual seismic shifts have been transpiring globally for decades, these missional movements have just started to register on the American Religious Richter Scale. According to a report issued by the Barna Group in January 2009, "50 percent of the adults interviewed agreed that Christianity is no longer the faith that Americans automatically accept as their personal faith." While the United States is just now seeing the first generation of adults who have been raised with no religious background, other parts of the world, such as Europe, Australia, and the UK, have been classified as post-Christian for decades. For example, at the start of the twentieth century, 80 percent of UK children attended church or Sunday school; by 2005, this number had fallen to 12 percent.

> *The era of Christianity as a Western religion is already over. Instead of "Western Christianity," we now witness a post-Christian West (in Europe) and a post-Western Christianity (in the global South). America is somewhere in between.*
>
> **Harvey Cox,** *The Future of Faith*

I have no clue what kind of theological tremors and faith faults will happen down the road or what the religious landscape will look like after these tectonic plates stop shifting. But if bloggers like Andrew Jones and Jonny Baker are spot-on, then I think it's safe to assume that we can expect to see some long-term spiritual shifts on the horizon that will be transpiring for generations to come. Seems to me there's much we can learn from our collective experiences moving forward, if we can find a way to turn down the volume and tune out the white noise so we can really start listening to each other.

Suffice it to say, I needed a break to digest these revelations. In lieu of using my MP3 recorder to document the slew of scholarly sessions, I chilled to some tunes I downloaded from Proost and this collection of spiritual songs:

"Always Look on the Bright Side of Life"	*Spamalot*
"American Jesus"	Bad Religion
"Black Jesus"	Everlast
"Heaven Is a Place on Earth"	Brenda Carlisle
"Holy Water"	Big & Rich
"Jesus Christ Is Still the King"	Billy Joe Shaver (Kinky Friedman's spiritual director)
"Jesus Loves Me (But He Can't Stand You)"	The Austin Lounge Lizards
"Missionary Man"	The Eurthymics
"Plastic Jesus"	Billy Idol
"Personal Jesus"	Marilyn Manson
"Son of a Preacher Man"	Dusty Springfield
"They Aren't Making Jews like Jesus Anymore"	Kinky Friedman
"The Vatican Rag"	Tom Lehrer

Somehow, this serious yet sacrilegious selection of music put me in a frame of mind where I was able to detach myself and actually laugh at the silly shtick I just witnessed. Fortunately, a session with N. T. Wright post-Soularize (sans Bermuda shorts of course) recharged my biblical batteries, while a reception honoring philosopher Huston Smith reminded me of the significant scholarship one can achieve by exploring other religions while remaining committed to one's own faith tradition.

After my avowed atheist brother showed up for my book launch, I honored his request to duck out of AAR/SBL early Monday morning to head for Las Vegas. In the spirit of trying to "be," I sat back and let the ethos of Las Vegas seep into me. Yuck, what a mess.

The majestic mountains surrounding Sin City are obliterated by massive man-made monstrosities. An endless parade of billboards promoting Celine Dion's final tour seemed to parallel the buzz generated by certain Christian commercial endeavors. Monied megachurch ministers Fred Price and Creflo Dollar could replace Penn and Teller as a prosperity puppet show. Heck, put a wig on Joel Osteen, and Celine could take the night off.

> *You con men, phonies, doing your religion for the celebrity ratings ... but you look fantastic.*
> **Rob Lacey,**
> *The Word on the Street*

The sickly sweet scent of cheap salvation lingered in the air. Move beyond the all-you-can-eat buffets, the free watered-down drinks, and the throngs of illegal aliens hawking flyers promising the ultimate sexual partner — this desert oasis is but a mirage.

Every casino lures you in with a glitzy gimmick, whether a Venetian gondola ride or a replica of Manhattan. However, once you get past the elegant exteriors, each casino seemed to follow the identical floor plan. Then it hit me — Emergent Church™, New Monasticism®, Organic Church©, and other new brands of Christianity look just like Las Vegas; the book covers may be different, but much of the content is the same. While these leaders might have read *Colossians Remixed*, instead of subverting the empire, they end up creating their own version of McChurch.

Like Elvis, Jesus has left the building. (Perhaps he's still around, but Judas locked him in a coin-operated toilet.) But one can find plenty of impersonators trying to simulate the real deal. Just as I can't see the natural Nevada beauty because my eyes are focused on the action taking place on the Strip, perhaps there's been so much "talk" about "doing" church that the still, quiet voice of God has been temporarily silenced.

This revelation would be sufficient to fill any pilgrim's notebook, but my trip wasn't over. Following the typical family Thanksgiving dinner, sans Hollywood-style hysterics (a major milestone for my family), I took my family to see *The Glory of Christmas* at the Crystal Cathedral.

When Robert Schuller, Inc., stages the birth of Christ, 228 seats have to be removed from the 2,736-seat Crystal Cathedral sanctuary to accommodate the Broadway-style set, which takes a month to prepare, partly because of the "angel track installation." That's right, angel tracks. That would be for the benefit of the eight angels who can go as high as eighty feet and travel as fast as twenty-five miles per hour. Then there are the three adult camels, one baby camel, six horses, a yak, a llama, a baby water buffalo, and untold numbers of sheep and goats onstage, along with the three hundred volunteer ushers and "actors." (The performers bringing this story to life seemed to possess the same earnestness and training of the performers I saw in action at Nazareth.)

The whole thing is staged to the accompaniment of the London Symphony Orchestra — well, a *recording* of the London Symphony Orchestra — resulting in what would best be described as a spectacle of the first two chapters of Luke as they would have been envisioned by Aimee Semple MacPherson if she had known about special effects.

They've been doing this show faithfully since 1981, one year after Schuller dedicated his glass-and-steel mega – office complex. This year, they ignored my connection to *The Wittenburg Door* and forked over tickets for my family, including my sixteen-year-old nephew, who assured me that, no matter how you swivel your neck, there's no way you can get a good look up the heavenly skirts of those flying angels, and my fourteen-year-old niece, who said the highlight for her was when the Roman soldier's horse relieved himself on the stage.

On our way out of the theater, we passed the In-Car Worship Center; a Christmas tree that could rival the one at Rockefeller Center; a spirit-filled gift shop that sold all things Crystal; and life-sized statues of major biblical figures, including Moses, the holy family on donkeys, and Jesus walking on water.

I didn't share my atheist family's assessment that the entire show was god-awful, but I can't say I was touched by it either, despite the comforting sound of Robert Schuller's recorded voice assuring me that "God loves you, and so do I." And I can't help but point out that this is one of the few churches that, at Christmastime, doesn't have some kind of a food donation box or some other means of donating to the less fortunate. Then again, maybe that's because Schuller, Inc., concluded that this show itself is what the  needy need. According to the Crystal Cathedral website, "Interested donors can give the gift of *The Glory of Christmas* to a needy child or organization this season."

And lest anyone miss out on basking in *The Glory of Christmas*, it's just three short months until the Crystal Cathedral resurrects *The Glory of Easter.* Nothing says Christ has risen like angel tracks.

After sampling AAR/SBL, Las Vegas, and the Crystal Cathedral, I got one heck of a spiritual stomachache. Fortunately, my press tickets for the Dead Sea Scrolls exhibit at the San Diego Museum of Natural History provided a theological Tums of sorts — finally, some religious relief. I had already seen these scrolls at the Shrine of the Book in Jerusalem and the Jordan Archaeological Museum. But this time I got to take my niece through this exhibit. As I illustrated for this budding artist how artisans before her had created work that continues to inspire us, I felt a theological tug that brought me back to the global spirit Diana Butler Bass illuminated for me the previous week.

Looking over the photos of Qumran and the Dead Sea, I was reminded that while we're supposed to be the salt of the earth (Matthew 5:13), if we lose touch with the Scriptures, then we get so salty all we can do is float. My challenge is to stay connected and grounded, regardless of what is transpiring around me. I can very easily get so caught up in critiquing emergent exercises, progressive power plays, and other ungodly games that I forget to follow the living Christ.

In every age, claims to possess unique (or at least superior) access to the HOLY are rife. Such claims are often entangled with struggles for power or financial gain, but they cannot simply be reduced to them. If anything, our desire to exceed one another in our "command" of ULTIMATE REALITY is even more decisive than the struggle for everyday goods.

L. William Countryman,
Living on the Border of the Holy

Mother Teresa Unplugged

DECEMBER 2007

After months of traveling almost nonstop, my feet finally touched ground in New York City. Home at last. I was so used to being on the go, go, go that standing still caught me off guard.

The sight of purple-clad priests, papier-mâché pageants, and storefront Santas reminded me that it was Christmastime. The folks at Alternatives for Simple Living, a grassroots group that helps people challenge rampant consumerism and celebrate responsibly, have shown me how to curtail my pre-Christmas activities (though I have yet to do Advent "right," whatever the heck that means).

During this time of darkness before Christ's birth, we're supposed to be waiting in anticipation for that moment when God comes into the world. But no matter how I try to get into the spiritual groove, I end up feeling restless and fidgety. It's like I'm coming down with a case of the Christian chiggers. Not life threatening, mind you, but annoying as all get-out.

As I sat there scratching and swearing, I received an unexpected package, a review copy of *Come Be My Light*. Mother Teresa requested that her personal correspondence to her spiritual director remain private; however, the papal powers decided to release her letters as part of her canonization process.

In her letters I discovered a stark honesty. Mother Teresa was not the woman we thought we knew. While the world put her on a pious pedestal (and a few snarky souls like Christopher Hitchens, author of *The Missionary Position: Mother Teresa in Theory and Practice*, kicked her to the curb), this seemingly simple nun from

Calcutta spent most of her ministry isolated and all alone. These letters indicate that ever since she began her ministry to the poor, the voice of Jesus that guided her to start this work became silent. Never again would she hear from the Jesus of her childhood, who had guided her thus far.

> Pray for me — for within me everything is icy cold. — It is only that blind faith that carries me through for in reality to me all is darkness. As long as our Lord has all the pleasure — I really do not count.

With a Joblike sense of determination, she learned to embrace this darkness as a part of her ministry.

> Let Him do with me whatever He wants as He wants for as long as He wants. If my darkness is light to some soul — even if it be nothing to nobody — I am perfectly happy — to be God's flower of the field.

Her living light that shone brightly to others even when all she could see was blackness gives me hope that God can work in me even when I can't see squat.

During Advent, I attended a press screening for *I Am Legend*. Despite the fact that Robert Neville (Will Smith) kept his body in top physical shape, his soul started to deteriorate under the pressures of living a solitary life. This demise of the self brought to mind the documentary *Soul Searching: The Journey of Thomas Merton*.

There's a little candle in me that, so far, has not gone out.

What struck me about Merton's journey was how his fellow Trappist monks provided the support that enabled him to live in community even though he spent much of his life in solitude.

For whatever reason, those leading the centering prayer groups that I participated in during the 1980s never introduced me to Merton's work. Even today, some who market themselves as cutting-edge thinkers pontificate on how "doubt is the new faith" as though they invented the concept. In his gentle yet persistent voice, Merton reminded me how questioning God has been an integral part of our spiritual DNA from the get-go.

For centuries, pilgrims like the Copts, the Celts, and the Chaldeans have followed God into this cloud of unknowing. Rather than reinvent the wheel, we might want to reinterpret the wisdom of those who came before us to see how they speak to us today. Perhaps we need a little less postmodernity and a lot more Merton.

> *My Lord God, I have no idea where I am going. I do not see the road ahead of me. I cannot know for certain where it will end. Nor do I really know myself, and the fact that I think I am following your will does not mean that I am actually doing so. But I believe that the desire to please you does in fact please you. And I hope I have that desire in all that I am doing. I hope that I will never do anything apart from that desire. And I know that if I do this you will lead me by the right road, though I may know nothing about it. Therefore I will trust you always though I may seem to be lost and in the shadow of death. I will not fear, for you are ever with me, and you will never leave me to face my perils alone.*
>
> **Thomas Merton,** *Thoughts in Solitude*

These days my community remains scattered around the globe. Like many writers, I do much of my work in isolation. Hence, I have to keep reminding myself that I might be by myself, but I'm not totally alone. Hard to do, though, when I reach out and no one is home — not even God. Or so it seems. Then again, we're in Advent, waiting for Christ to come into the world. As I discovered in Petra, Joseph and Mary could always count on the donkey to lead them to God.

Good without God

WINTER 2008

I almost circular-filed my invitation to the screening of the documentary *A Purple State of Mind*. I really didn't know if I could witness another Angry Atheist vs. Clueless Christian smackdown. All too often, the voice of reason gets silenced when these bestselling bullies whip up their respective crowds into a feeding frenzy.

Still, my inner voice that never shuts the heck up told me to go to this screening. Much to my pleasant surprise, I was treated to an honest and humorous dialogue between John Marks and Craig Detweiler, former college roommates. The Orwellian year 1984 marked the beginning of Craig's faith and the last year of John's. After this fateful year, the two men went their separate ways. The film picks up on their conversation some twenty-five years later.

At first, I struggled with the depiction of Christianity portrayed by these guys. As a budding writer, I was far too geeky to be a

SCIENCE AND RELIGION FINALLY AGREE.

119

high-school-athlete-turned-Christian-missionary like Craig. Nor did I have that beautiful-as-Barbie Christian lifestyle that John eventually left behind. For starters, my dogs ate my Barbies (except during Advent, when they preferred to chomp down on the figurines in our stable). My childhood was more Felliniesque than fairy tale.

As the documentary progressed, I began to see how these men's stories paralleled many of my own struggles. Like them, I often wondered where God was in the midst of global conflicts and my own personal pain. As a religious satirist, I've known more than my fair share of spiritual swindlers. Fortunately, I have a few trusted old souls in my life who have convinced me to keep walking forward on this admittedly dark spiritual path.

While neither Craig nor John compromised their beliefs, these former college buddies were able to have a conversation of the heart. Despite glaring differences on matters of faith, their friendship enabled them to move beyond the yelling matches generated by extremists in both camps and explore the common ground of their shared humanity. In particular, I was struck by how Craig just sat and listened to John's tearful confession that he could no longer believe in God after what he witnessed while covering the Bosnian war. Many Christians would have walked away when John renounced his childhood faith, citing that as believers they could not cavort with an unclean sinner who is no longer Bible blessed. But Craig chose to be left behind by remaining friends with John in spite of their theological differences.

Unfortunately, these genuine dialogues remain few and far between. So when I connected with Greg Epstein, the humanist chaplain of Harvard University, as part of my research for my book *The New Atheist Crusaders and Their Unholy Grail*, I felt I had met a kindred spirit of sorts. We've both witnessed our share of shouting matches in which both New Atheists and certain Christians focused all of their energies into converting the other and flaming their perceived "enemies" instead of seeking out areas of cooperation around issues such as caring for the environment, ending sex trafficking, and keeping church and state as separate entities. (Interesting how "the other" always ends up being those who don't look or act like those we consider to be part of our inner circle.)

Now, I'm not proposing a wishy-washy, anything-goes scenario where Christians park their faith at the door. I've seen too many attempts at interfaith dialogue in which, in the name of tolerance, a group of religious leaders representing the extreme-left factions gather together at some conference, panel discussion, or other academic enterprise. (Once again, more moderate voices tend to be noticeably absent from these conversations.) Under the guise of inclusivity and tolerance, these groups produce some universalist peace-and-harmony manifesto that doesn't really do justice to the tenets of the different faiths present. This God goo enables everyone to feel good about themselves because they "did something" to advance the cause of interfaith dialogue and cooperation. But for all their talk, their actual programming lacks any practical application whatsoever.

I witnessed a small example of how we can move past our prejudices and our distrust of others to work together for a common good when I viewed the film *Call + Response*. This chilling documentary exposes the world's dirtiest secret: There are more slaves today than at any other time in human history. The Not For Sale campaign, one of the driving forces behind this documentary, brings together a wide swath of people, including faith groups, students, teachers, artists, consumers, and businesspeople, in support of this common issue. Such coalition building can only happen when we truly seek to engage others in grassroots activism without trying to convert them into Christian soldiers.

Maybe the great challenge is to trust so much in God's love that I don't have to be afraid to enter fully into the secular world and speak there about faith, hope, and love. Maybe the place where that gap has to be bridged is within me.
Henri Nouwen, *Life of the Beloved*

Holy Hippies

WINTER 2008

All I know about Hartsville, South Carolina, is that my birth certificate says I was born there. My father, a child prodigy, graduated from college at nineteen, was ordained a deacon at twenty-two, and became the youngest priest in the Diocese of North Carolina. He was definitely the talk of the Carolina Country Club and touted by the bishop bigwigs as "the next big theological thing." When he moved to Hartsville to become rector of St. Bartholomew's Episcopal Church at the tender age of twenty-five, my socialite granny bragged about her son till her bubble burst.

By the time he turned thirty, Dad finally stopped dating Southern debutantes and dignitaries' daughters. He settled down and married Nancy Williams Little (a direct descendant of Roger Williams and three pilgrims from the *Mayflower*). Depending on which family member you ask, Dad settled for a damn Yankee or Mom married a Southern snot — either way my extended family viewed my parents as black sheep who had no business intermingling with the more purebred lambs.

Since I was orphaned before I turned seventeen, I've wondered what really happened during the period of my life when my parents' addictions started to outrun their idealism. My family kept me at bay until I turned twenty-one. Then I was deemed old enough to learn the family secrets. Thus began my mis-education. Facts and fables were grafted onto my dysfunctional family tree until my genealogical chart looked like Jackson Pollock had gone gonzo with his paints, cigarette butts soaked in whiskey, and bits of doo-doo.

Colorful, yes, but it really stank.

One day I received an unexpected email from one of Dad's former parishioners. Finally a bit of clarity to clear up my confusion.

Here's how I came to know your father. My husband and I joined his church. In his first years, Karl was a much-loved rector, largely because he was regarded as a lovable person. I still remember unpolished loafers peeking from under his black robe as I took Communion. They were the kind of foible that parishioners found forgivable, even charming in a boyish way. One of Karl's favorite hymns was Martin Luther's "A Mighty Fortress." I can visualize the thrust of his strong jaw as he sang it in the processional. I wonder what that choice of hymn says about him and if it remained a favorite.

We started working with Karl's youth group. We often visited him in the rectory late at night after I finished my studies. Karl was always wide-awake and delighted to have company. We'd sit for an hour or so and talk, laugh, whatever. I remember a raucous rendition of "Let the Good Times Roll" and of being introduced to the satirical song stylings of Tom Lehrer.

Her recollections of Dad's humor ring true. How many nine-year-olds can recite both the Lord's Prayer and the lyrics to "The Vatican Rag"? Humor became my saving grace as I grew up in a household that seemed ill-fated from the get-go.

When I did the

math, I realized that if my mother got married when she was eighteen, my parents started dating when she was underage. Those sounds you hear ringing in your ears are the warning bells of reason. It's odd that no one thought it weird that the rector was dating a teenager from his youth group — but no one knew they were an item.

> Your mom and dad dated "secretively" while she was still in high school. Though there wasn't the consciousness of abuse that we have today, they both knew parishioners would not think it was a good idea for them to date. I remember one story of your mom hiding behind the front seat of the car so she wouldn't be seen.

> I don't know why her mother went along with this. Maybe it was a vicarious thing to distract her from the loss of her husband. The marriage did put a stop to Nancy's education. I remember Nancy telling me that she planned to read and to educate herself through reading rather than through pursuit of a degree. Karl and her mother seemed to think that would be a great idea. I treasured my college education so much that I was quite dubious about it, but I didn't argue.

After Mom's dad died, her mother began to lose herself in liquor. When I was at Yale Divinity School, I ran into someone who worked as one of my grandma's work-study students. She seemed to have sobered up enough to get a degree in library sciences. He told me how warm and loving she was toward him, adding that one of his highlights was when they attended the nearby Episcopal church together and she'd have him over for dinner afterward. I never had the privilege of seeing this grandmotherly compassion up close and personal.

I can see now how my mother wandered around Hartsville like a lost spiritual sheep. Such a lonely soul could become very susceptible to the charms of a holy man who had a gift to touch outcasts and bring them into his fold. I still remember a story she told me about Dad's first confirmation class. Just as the bishop started the laying on of hands, a dove flew in, circled the altar, and left. Those present felt touched by the hand of God. But alongside tales of spiritual transformation, she hinted at other "laying on of hands" stories that proved that Dad had his share of starstruck coeds. I was never told all the sordid details, though from what I can piece together, my bisexual father appeared to resemble that classic saint-turned-sexual-sinner character one finds far too often in Christian circles. He could serve as a textbook case for what happens when the charismatic cult of personality runs roughshod over the gospel. Mixing together sex and spirituality with an added alcohol chaser produces one heck of a toxic cocktail that is best not sipped or even stirred.

Mom regaled me with stories of Dad's civil rights activism. I lost track of the number of times she told me about their trek to Greensboro, where they joined the Woolworth's lunch counter sit-in. It was as though she was a former high school cheerleader, reliving her glory days, thinking her life had stopped moving after graduation.

According to family lore, troubles ensued when my father began preaching about the need to invite Negroes to worship at this lily-white church. He was trying to build a bridge that no one wanted to cross. This was the Deep South pre-1964, when one could lose one's life for daring to preach that all have a right to enter the Promised Land. Seems the other area ministers chose to side with the people of Hartsville, who thought it was A-OK to blow off *Brown v. Board of Education.*

> I do think some of the problems with the Hartsville congregation came partly because Karl got to be a one-note preacher. He was so obsessed with civil rights that he preached on it every Sunday. They might have been better able to accept or at least deal with integration if he had also spoken about other spiritual subjects.

> I do wonder, though, just how he intended to integrate St. Bartholomew's. There wasn't a black Episcopal congregation in the area. Also, African Americans have a distinctive worship style that differs radically from white congregational practices. Some of my African-American high school students

at Wilson High School in Florence, South Carolina, asked me questions like, "Do y'all sing those dull, draggy hymns?" and "Have you ever felt the Holy Spirit?" I don't think it's likely they would have come even if they were invited. If Karl wanted to integrate the church, how would he have gone about it? Or did he just promote the *idea* of integration?

Eventually Dad was forced out of town by the Ku Klux Klan, who were taking notes on his sermons and calling the rectory late at night. The next and last time Dad's former parishioner met my father, the Golden Boy seems to have lost his luster.

In the mid-sixties, we connected with your family at the beach. During that visit, Karl seemed very different from the Karl we had known earlier. He still had the twinkly eyes, the ebullience, but he seemed to be moving in a direction that we didn't connect with.

She didn't connect with Dad partly because he had tuned out by doing LSD with Timothy Leary. (This remains one of the creepier tidbits thrust on me as an adult.) Apparently these forward thinkers thought they could expand their minds and create heaven here on earth. Buddy Jesus was seen as a fellow hippie traveler. Think of him as the drug runner who delivered the fuel that fed their faith.

I followed my father's hazy history to Duke University, where he got his PhD in sociology. After some digging, I found the abstract of his dissertation, titled "The Tyranny of Freedom: A Study of Dimensions of the Sacred in the Development of an Activist Sectarian Enterprise (1968)."

The psychedelic experience is a powerful experience, but it does not end with the experience. What happens next? How do we live our lives? What happens after the ecstasy? We see the world in a different way, but what do we do with that realization?

Don Lattin, *The Harvard Psychedelic Club*

HIPPIE HOLY DAZE

SINGER

During the same time period I was dropping out of kindergarten and feeding the swans on the Boston Commons, Dad spent his days researching the totalitarianism that emerged from radical countercultural groups. As I was reading this abstract, I was struck by how my father's analysis of radical communities like the Students for Democratic Society (SDS) and some religious groups back in the 1960s parallels many of the discussions happening today around the formation of post-Christian communities. Individuals on the outskirts of society became attracted to radical groups that promised a utopian society. They bonded together by their common concerns and beliefs, whether religious, political, or cultural. As Dad's research noted, what originated as an idealistic communitarian group soon developed into a de facto organization with a hierarchy of sorts. When left unchecked, these power dynamics transformed into a horror show that would give even Wes Craven the willies.

My mind was reeling, so I asked the Rev. Kurt Neilson, my pilgrim guide, for his astute analysis. As always, he delivered in spades.

I find it's a fascinating "period" document. He clearly had great respect for the SDS (Students for a Democratic Society) folks, while he was trying to do some sort of objective treatment of how they dealt with one another and how paradoxical was the shift into unilateral dogmatism in a group with "democratic" ideology. I even detected a hint of a note of fear. As we know, the more radical fringe of SDS was demonstrating its capacity for violence, and I wonder if he feared for himself or for his family by doing this work. He also hinted, I thought, at the cost to his family life exacted by hanging with these folks at their gatherings. But there was a note of respectful regard for SDS and a desire to take them and their ideals seriously. Your heritage, if I may be so bold, from both the recent and the distant past, is one of passionate idealism willing to take risks.

Sure, sixties-era songs can sound pretty goofy when sung today. But at the time, these lyrics had real meaning because they represented a fresh way of looking at the world. These hippies truly thought they could change the world. But as my father demonstrated, by 1968, the year they lost Bobbie and Martin, the dream died. These pseudo-radicals turned inward and, in some cases, imploded.

According to my parents, Dad's unsuccessful attempts to secure a tenured professorship and a chichi church gig could be attributed to a variety of factors, including, but by no means limited to, their parents, the Vietnam War, the Garrison kids (especially when we fought in front of high-ranking university personnel), Nixon, the next-door neighbor, Sirhan Sirhan, faculty wives, Governor Wallace, the local PTA, the Episcopal Church, brownnosing students, and even our dog, Sunshine. They never comprehended the reality that perhaps institutions might not want to hire an aging enfant terrible who kept staging *Lord of the Flies* – type scenarios against "the man," while expecting the establishment to fund his Jackesque behavior.

Writer Merrill Markoe describes these kinds of people as narcissists who "cover up feelings of shame and worthlessness inflicted during their own screwy childhoods by doing whatever it takes to maintain a false sense that they are very special and therefore not bound by ordinary rules." She offers an insightful explanation for why people like my late father tend to act in this manner:

Narcissists essentially live in a world that is one person big because they never fully outgrow a phase of infantile behavioral development in which baby thinks he and Mommy are the same person.... When you are with a narcissist, their needs must become your needs. It's not enough for a narcissist to be the center of his own world; he must also be the center of yours.

Imbued with the spirit of self-righteousness, narcissists like my dad deceive themselves into believing their desires are in sync with Jesus' call for their lives. The Lord's Prayer asking God that *his* will be done is replaced by "God bless *my* will."

Welcome to my family's party of one where I assumed the role of the unwelcome guest.

They floated down the river of denial as I pointed out the white elephants, asking why so many of my relatives were drunk. They kept telling me that they were "resting" and other euphemisms to conceal the stone-cold reality that my entire family was pretty much passed out. It was almost as though Monty Python's "Dead Parrot" sketch was being reenacted right in front of me.

Then the U.S. government started parroting platitudes. In response, my family attended folk festivals and protested against the Vietnam War. My father took us to see a student play about Jesus, the righteous rocker. As if to demonstrate subconsciously just how far his faith had fallen, Dad had a minor role as the "pig" who arrested this long-haired hippie freak.

I joined in Dad's artistic anarchy by writing a one-act political play that pretty much crucified Tricky Dick while setting up Ted Kennedy as the next Messiah. (This was before I taught myself how to spell Chappaquiddick.) Whenever Richard Milhous Nixon's mug would appear on the television set, this nine-year-old would give the screen the middle finger. My parents applauded my antipatriotism. They were all for peace, love, and tolerance, but their rants against the "*&^%$*! establishment" showed they didn't exactly practice what they preached.

> *For God so loved the world that he gave his one and only Son, that whoever believes in him shall not perish but have eternal life.*
> **John 3:16**

Their definition of *activism* never included any talk about *agape* (Matthew 22:34–40; Mark 12:28–34). To this day, I wonder why my late parents were so full of self-righteous anger that they never taught me how Jesus dealt with his enemies.

Dad overloaded his Sunday sermons with countercultural slogans that were full of tolerance but light on theology. Without the power of the risen Christ, Dad's civil rights activism that drew him to seek the priesthood was reduced to Sesame Street sing-alongs. When peaceful progressives downplay the life-transforming power of the resurrection, they reduce the words of "social justice" Jesus to just another prophetic voice calling people to repent.

Even though Christian marketers give John 3:16 a bad name — can I interest you in a John 3:16 gem-studded prayer bear? — I still get chills down my spine when I reflect on this verse. I just can't comprehend why the Creator of all, who loves all of his creation unconditionally, would bring his Son into the world to suffer, die, and then rise from the dead unless he knew such an act was needed to transform the world.

Still, there are times when one can feel that the story ends at the foot of the cross, abandoned and all alone.

A few months before my mother overdosed in the summer of 1978, I remember sitting with her as some sixties documentary played in the background. Her eyes filled with tears. "You're a dreamer. So was your dad. That's not good. You want things that aren't possible."

I sought ordination in some subconscious quest to fulfill my father's dream. But I soon realized I was way too much of a smarty-pants to ever get collared in. My talents clearly lay as a lone wolf holding a mirror up to the institutional church, not a shepherd pasturing her flock or a visionary leading a forward-thinking nonprofit. Whereas Dad blamed his parents for his demise, I admit to my own neuroses. However, I do see how this familial thread weaves itself throughout my life. Every so often, I still find myself trying to help yet another narcissistic genius filled with all the potential and promise. As much as I might be attracted to their charismatic vision, I try to walk away whenever their talk of "community" sounds more self-centered than Christlike.

Thankfully, God's grace breaks through all of this personal baggage. In my twenties, some Christians entered my life who gave me the love and guidance that my alcoholic parents could not give me. Without these ordinary angels, I suspect I would have joined my parents in pushing up daisies. I didn't realize until recently how blessed I was to have these people come into my life. When church communities see someone in psychic pain, I've noticed they have a tendency to either gossip about the fallen sinner or play ostrich in the hopes that the problem will resolve itself with prayer. Instead of being guided toward the lifelong road to recovery, the person implodes, leaving behind considerable damage to both themselves and others.

> *While many sounds can hurt our ears, I think silence is the most painful because it can hurt our hearts.*
> **Margaret Feinberg,**
> *The Sacred Echo*

I joke that because I've been to hell and back, I can serve as a tour guide for others. I try not to make the distinction between inner child/outer adult because, thanks to souls like Mike Yaconelli, I haven't really "grown up" in the conventional sense of the term, and odds are I never will. The essence of the inner child means that, despite the horrors and hells we've experienced, we never stop giggling when something tickles our funny bone, even if that means we're laughing all by ourselves.

Karl Barth had it right when he summarized his teachings with the simple yet profound statement "Jesus loves me, this I know." Before anyone starts accusing this German heavyweight of becoming more Barneyesque than Barthian (hard to do when *Church Dogmatics* weighs in at a hefty fourteen volumes!), he's not doing some happy-happy-joy-joy devotional dance. Rather, he's revealing the power of the resurrection, the transformative love of the risen Christ that no earthly power can destroy.

The More Things Change ...

April was indeed the cruelest month. My satirical sensibilities were tested to the limits from April 18 to 20, when both the New York Comic Con and the Papal Visit came to the Big Apple. For three glorious days, the faithful flocked into Manhattan to pay homage to their beloved superhero, whether Hellboy or His Holiness.

Talk about a full-scale frontal assault on American popular culture. Both sides wore their armor and sharpened their weapons. Will the graphic novel kick some sacrilegious butt, or will the papal encyclical come from behind and go all medieval on the Lords of Darkness? The tension mounted as crowds lined up behind the greatest artist in comic book history (Stan Lee) and the second most popular pope of the last four years (Benedict XVI). Unfortunately, those expecting a bit of Armageddon action were left behind. The Popemobile steered clear of the Javits Center, depriving us of the chance to witness Star Wars Stormtroopers crossing paths with the Pope's Secret Service.

Shortly after Stan Lee and Pope Benedict bade farewell to their fawning fans, Brian McLaren, one of *Time* magazine's Top 25 Evangelicals, arrived in town to headline the Bronx leg of his Everything

Must Change tour. For those who wish to crown Brian "the emergent emperor," methinks he would prefer to be known as Brian "the bridge builder" (not to be confused with Bob the Builder).

The original title for Brian's book *Everything Must Change* was *Jesus and the Suicide Machine*, a fact that brings home the point that Brian feels we're in the midst of a global calamity, especially in terms of the environment and our military muscle. After a collaborative meditative process, Deep Shift was formed to address this crisis. Say "Deep Shift" really fast ten times, and you get the gist of what Brian believes will happen if Christians don't make some major shifts in their priorities immediately.

When I arrived at this event, we all greeted each other with the usual "Bless you, sister," and "I'll pray for you." This God-talk sounds like the religious equivalent of "Have a nice day" and "How are you?" Often in Christian circles we utter pastoral pleasantries, but God forbid we should engage with each other. Actually telling people what's on our minds would involve stepping in some deep shift that I sense most of us would rather avoid. For the most part, I respond in kind, as though I'm on religious autopilot. So I'm guilty of contributing to these faux faith feelings more often than I'd like to admit.

If we say we love God yet hate a brother or sister, we are liars. For if we do not love a fellow believer, whom we have seen, we cannot love God, whom we have not seen.

1 John 4:20

Ritual stations were set up so the participants could write down notes, pray before a cross, touch some dirt, cleanse oneself in water, and even get anointed with oil. When I walked by these stations, I had this Anglican authority sneer in my soul. This all looked homemade, and I couldn't help thinking that evangelicals never seem to do ritual "right."

But when I looked into the water, I saw a reflection that frankly scared me. Who the heck is this angry chick? I truly needed to be reborn. Righteous anger, which is one of the best weapons in the satirist's arsenal, can eat me alive if I'm not careful. Jesus must look at some of my moves and shake his head. Time after time, I fail to put the Greatest Commandment into practice. As much as I want to be the humble tax collector, I often come off as the self-righteous, judgmental Pharisee (Luke 18:10–12). I hate when I get in the way. I keep forgetting that God works through broken vessels, including me.

Brian asked Jay Bakker, pastor of Revolution Church, and me to give a five-minute response to his first talk. I puffed up a perfect response to a few progressive partisans and misbehaving missionals I saw scattered throughout the crowd. But then I sat and pondered Brian's question, "Which Jesus do we follow?" When I stood up, I wasn't sure what I would say, but something told me to lay off the theological trash talk.

I began by connecting Brian's slide show of his trip to Israel with my experience witnessing Condi's U.S. State Department–sanctioned caravan in Jerusalem. That sight reminded me how select Christians have appointed Jesus Christ to the rank of a four-star general in the "War on Terror." Meanwhile, some progressives depict Jesus of Nazareth as the ultimate social justice warrior, as though they've reduced the crucifixion to nothing more than a really bad day at the activist office. Then you have those armchair insurrectionists decked out in faux Che Guevara gear who deconstruct and then deny the resurrection, a war of words that may exercise the mind but fails to feed the soul. All this cherry-picking through the gospel leaves us with a Christ that tastes good but in the end is less filling.

Then I recalled the church sign that someone made for the Mike Yaconelli memorial tribute website. It read, "Mike Yaconelli was a dangerous, messy man. Our carpets are proof of it." Like the archangel Gabriel, who scared the bejesus out of the Virgin Mary back in Nazareth, Mike's call for us to follow the real Jesus really frightens me at times. Are those of us present at this event prepared to be shaken, not stirred?

To Brian's credit, I see some deep shifts starting to happen this weekend. His worship leader and cochairs are women. In addition, he chose the Latino Action Pastoral Center and the Latino Leadership Circle as the lead New York City sponsors. Also, he arranged for other authors' books to be displayed, as well as literature from a range of grassroots organizations. So there's more of a communal feel here than what I usually find at most author events.

Still, if everything must change for us to save ourselves and our planet, when will this start to have a transformative impact on our church communities? For example, the "emergent" video shown consisted mostly of white males "talking" about "doing" church. Looks like the deep shift hit the fan a bit there. Also, we're in the Bronx, and yet the gathering looked lily-white to me.

Like Lilly Von Schtupp, the female heroine of sorts in *Blazing Saddles*, I'm tired. Sick and tired of people preaching about ushering in this new kingdom of God, when their programs attract mostly well-educated males with only a smattering of minorities. Once in a blue moon, one can find a gathering that's more female friendly. These women's gatherings tend to remind me of my debutante and Junior League days, where the women get to be displayed on center stage. But do the math, and it's pretty clear that in this game, women are just the players — the men still own the chessboard.

Perhaps those of us on the outside should stop trying to sit at the head table. It's pretty obvious that these gatekeepers aren't going to let us in, no matter how hard we try to crash their conferences. Let's throw our own faith festivals instead.

"I can't stand your religious meetings. I'm fed up with your conferences."
(God, Amos 5:23)

©dhayward

It's high time that when we all gather together in his name, we reflect his people. Otherwise, all our talk about unifying the church is just that. If I sound jaded, it's because I heard all this peace and unity jazz from my late father. But except for inviting a Native American to join us for a Thanksgiving dinner and hanging around with a few Black Panther types, he attracted a group of fairly homogeneous college-educated hippies. (These are the same types who protested against "da man," only to turn into tenured professors who preached political correctness to the next generation of college students, thus becoming that which they once despised once they got into a position of power.)

Yes, one can get a spiritual buzz at any gathering of the faithful, but I am wondering how we can all be as shrewd as snakes and innocent as doves in deciding where we invest our time and energies (Matthew 10:16). Not all buzzes are Bible blessed.

Are those gathered doing more than just contextualizing their faith, blogging beyond belief, and engaging in other postmodern ponderings? Often, I could get the same speeches via a live web conference, especially if participants can join in the conversation in real time through online tools such as Twitter and text messaging. (Along those lines, perhaps we should all recalculate our expense accounts and carbon footprints in light of the ongoing economic and environmental crises.)

This Westernized conference model consisting of speakers and passive participants seems to appeal mostly to postgraduate players. You can adjust things a bit with a more youthful and relevant lineup of speakers. Then throw in a few workshops and maybe some hands-on activities for some spiritual spice. But the end result isn't likely to appeal to those who encounter the holy through less talky methods, especially if they happen to be from non-Western European backgrounds.

Also, very few Christians regularly fly first or even economy class. Heck, I can't afford the money or the time to attend the vast majority of invites that cross my desk. So I try to focus my energy and limited finances on festivals that bring together a wide swath of people from different cultures for one giant communal party.

Let's be honest. If we're truly interested in "being the church," then maybe we need to stop conference hopping quite so much and look around our neighborhoods. What keeps us from participating in local festivals, block parties, church suppers, potlucks in people's homes, and whatever else they're doing? After all, this is how the upside-down kingdom of God works. Just as the king opened up his banquet to those deemed unworthy to sit anywhere near his majesty, Jesus commands us to go beyond our Christian comfort zones and welcome those viewed as undesirable by our secular society (Matthew 22:1 – 10; Luke 14:16 – 24).

Something tells me efforts to change this un-missional model will involve stepping in some really deep shift. After all, according to the gospel of Mark, James and John, the sons of Zebedee, requested to sit at Jesus' left and right hands (Mark 10:35 – 45). Matthew takes this request one step further by having the mother intercede on behalf of her sons, thus setting the stage for a slew of Jewish mama's-boy jokes (Matthew 20:20 – 28). Looks like this quest for recognition and power has been hitting the faith since the get-go.

Here I confess to being guilty more times than I care to admit of buying into someone's blog buzz. (Amazing how anyone can slap some leafy logo on their site and call themselves a "pastor" when their church consists only of their cat.) The anonymity of the Internet allows us to puff ourselves up. After I took a fast from Facebook during Lent 2009, I could see clearly that I had put far too much effort into creating a cool online persona instead of focusing on my inner prayer life.

Whenever I see communal ministries morph into a one-man pastor parade, I can get so religiously rabid in exposing "spiritual shams" that I can come off as overzealous and overbearing. One day when I was whining about some postmodern poser to Kurt Neilson, he pulled out a "Get Out of Gamaliel" card by quoting this wise Pharisee's words: "If their purpose or activity is of human origin, it will fail. But if it is from God, you will not be able to stop these men; you will only find yourselves fighting against God" (Acts 5:38 – 39).

So that I can be mindful when I've crossed that line from satirizing the subject at hand to slamming someone's soul, I've gathered a small group of pilgrims around me who represent a wide range of faith traditions. This informal accountability group reminds me when I have gone too far in my critiques and encourages me to work whenever possible to seek forgiveness and reconciliation, for as Jesus said, "Where two or three come together in my name, there am I with them" (Matthew 18:20).

I must confess that such a process can get quite messy. Seldom do reconciliations proceed step-by-step. Only in TV Land can intense interpersonal conflicts be solved in less than thirty minutes.

But if I claim to be a follower of Christ, then I have to take that first step and say, "I'm sorry." In some instances, my apology gets accepted and we can begin to repair our relationship. We may never be friends, but we can at least try to be in fellowship. In other cases, the pain I caused, albeit unintentionally, may have been too great. I place those situations in God's hands in the hope we can be reconciled over time through prayer.

As Paul preaches:

Therefore, if anyone is in Christ, the new creation has come: The old has gone, the new is here! All this is from God, who reconciled us to himself through Christ and gave us the ministry of reconciliation: that God was reconciling the world to himself in Christ, not counting people's sins against them.

And he has committed to us the message of reconciliation. We are therefore Christ's ambassadors, as though God were making his appeal through us. We implore you on Christ's behalf: Be reconciled to God.

2 CORINTHIANS 5:17–20

My prayer moving forward is that I remember when I pick up my pen that I must keep my eye on the prize.

Remembering Rightly

MAY 18, 2008

When I heard raindrops hitting my bedroom window, I thought about spending the day cocooned under the covers. Did I really want to endure a two-hour subway ride to Coney Island when the weather seemed more bluesy than beachlike?

But the Brooklyn Wall of Remembrance, a memorial to those firefighters and police officers who died on September 11, 2001, was being rededicated. I volunteered during the recovery effort, and while I've whittled down my involvement in post-9/11-related ministries considerably, I feel a pull to pay my respects on occasion. So I dragged my sleepy self out of bed and got dressed. A few hours later, I arrived at KeySpan Park, drenched.

According to one of the religious leaders who spoke, the rain meant God was crying for all those who perished while defending our freedoms. (The Lord's tears seem to be a better meteorological metaphor than my parents' joking that rain means God's peeing, and attributing hail, thunder, and other weather eruptions to other ungodly bodily functions.)

As the service began winding down, I bumped into a wounded veteran I met via the Achilles Track Club, a group that enables those with disabilities to participate in sporting activities. She's every bit the lady, with painted toenails on her prosthetic leg, but don't be deceived; she could kick my behind — and probably yours too. Thanks to the folks at Achilles, she completed her first New York City Marathon last year.

I tend to go for a kinder, gentler race, such as the Tunnel to Towers 5K Run/Walk. On September 11, 2001, FDNY firefighter

Stephen Siller ran in full bunker gear from the Brooklyn-Battery Tunnel to the World Trade Center, where he lost his life trying to save others. His family decided to honor his legacy by hosting an annual run/walk and block party that brings together over 20,000 firefighters and civilians from around the world to celebrate his life and raise money for the Stephen Siller FDNY "Let Us Do Good" Children's Foundation.

While I try to maintain my objectivity at these kinds of events, sometimes I get sloppy and sentimental. (You'll find me wearing sunglasses at a Habitat for Humanity home dedication because I lose it every time I see a kid jumping up and down for joy that he finally gets to live in his very own home.) Once again I found myself fighting back tears when I reflected on all those whose lives have been transformed post-9/11, both in the United States and around the world. Here go the sunglasses yet again so folks won't see me cry.

I also had to fight back a sudden and almost uncontrollable urge to smack some sense into our so-called political leaders. How many soldiers, firefighters, and other everyday heroes need to pull a John 15:13 ("Greater love has no one than this: to lay down one's life for one's friends") while our government, which sent them into battle, fails to provide for them and their families? When are we going to stop calling innocent women, men, and children "collateral damage"?

The sun came out just after the service ended. Draw your own cheesy analogy about God smiling. I went off to Nathan's, a Coney Island landmark, for a serving of clam strips. This treat might not be good for my cholesterol, but it was much needed for my soggy soul.

Jesus Sent Joe

JUNE 7, 2008

I should be more disciplined, more temperate, more grown-up. I should be more Christian, I suppose, whatever that means.

Cathleen Falsani, *Sin Boldly*

Some days, I can be quite the biblical baby. Take early June in New York City, for example. An unexpected heat wave blanketed the city, thus drenching us in a collective pool of sweat and stink.

I was riding home that day in a semi-air-conditioned subway car sandwiched next to other weatherworn souls.

Every time I travel anywhere, I'm approached by people looking for the time, needing directions, and wanting to engage in chit-chit.

"Where can I find the Soup Nazi?"

"Do you have the time?"

"Which subway do I take to get to Ground Zero?"

Normally I smile and respond to their requests, but that day I was in no mood to be nice. I hunkered down with my nose in a book, hoping I'd be left alone. But the combo of giddy girls discussing their sexual conquests, beat boys behaving badly, and cranky children rendered me unable to read and reflect. The title of the book in my hand: *Jesus Brand Spirituality.*

I'd like to say that some divine message entered me as I put the book down and tried to "be," but all I got was one unholy headache. Instead of being filled with Jesus-brand spirituality, I was OD'ing on self-righteous rubbish.

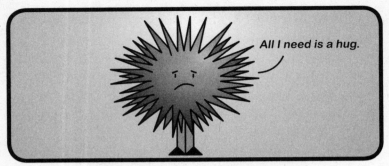

Would you dare?

Grace was noticeably absent. (My guess is she left the subway car looking for anything air-conditioned.)

A few days later, I ventured into All Angels Church on Manhattan's Upper West Side, my body still coated with a thick layer of subway stink. I used to worship here in the eighties, back when I was really into the Episcopal charismatic movement, and every so often I stop by for their Sunday evening jazz service.

During the prayers of the people, we were asked to turn to somebody next to us and share our prayer concerns. Asking an Anglican to talk about one's personal prayer life in public violates all that is frozen and chosen. We're more likely to prance around the pews stark naked than we are to bare our souls.

A man turned to me. I was stuck. My Southern sensibilities wouldn't permit me to follow my gut instinct, which was to pretend I had to go to the restroom. That would be just out-and-out rude. Joe looked a bit disheveled, but he didn't really stand out in particular on a hot summer day in New York City when we all looked more than a tad gamey.

Joe's prayer was simple: Help me through the day. Let me find a safe place to sleep tonight.

When he asked me about my prayer concerns, I was embarrassed as all get-out. Yes, my life was kind of messy. (So what else is new?) But my piddly prayer requests paled in comparison with Joe's simple needs. I just mumbled that he'd pray for me to find peace and left it at that.

Once again, God got the last laugh. Joe came to me as the hand of God (or more likely the Almighty's foot giving me a swift kick in the behind).

In watching Joe shuffle off after the community meal, I flashed back to a question that has haunted me for years. In my short-lived quest for ordination, I recall an afternoon I spent with a group of fellow aspirants being grilled by the Commission on Ministry. We were asked, "How do you handle problem people [read: the homeless] who come into your service and disrupt everyone's worship?" Immediately the group switched into problem-solving mode, offering their solutions for how they would deal with such annoyances.

After a few minutes, I stood up. "Wait. Excuse me, but I have a real issue with calling children of God 'problems.' After all, aren't we all broken and in need of God's grace?" I told the story of Fredericka, a mentally challenged woman who survived a Holocaust camp but since then had been hanging on by less than a thread. She attended church regularly, though we never knew how much of Fredericka was present on any given day. Her running commentary during the sermons was distracting at best. But after she died, her silence left a gaping hole. Upon her death, the rector told us that this frail old lady walked considerably more city blocks than I did just so she could be with us. Like the story of the widow's mite, she gave all she had to God (Mark 12:41–44; Luke 21:1–4).

In hindsight, this was probably the moment they concluded I was unordainable, as I can't be trusted to keep my big yap shut. Throughout church history, feisty women like Mary Magdalene, Joan of Arc, and Anne Hutchinson get dismissed as damaged or deranged by male-dominated religious structures determined to keep their voices at bay. While a church full of smart alecks would

Francis doubled his pleasure, doubled his fun.

149

be more provocative than pastoral, the church needs a few satirists around to keep her grounded, as well as mystics to give her hope. But all too often, the church assumes a used-car-salesman approach in selecting her leaders by promoting slick seminarians without bothering to check what's under their hoods.

Why do we embrace the St. John of the Crosses of yesteryear but dismiss those who exhibit similar traits today? Let's take a look at, say, St. Francis of Assisi, one of Christendom's all-time favorite saints. Would this saint be accepted in today's churches? Doubt it.

On a lark, I did a full psych workup on this favorite Franciscan for *The Wittenburg Door*. My preliminary diagnosis revealed a person who would have made Freud freak and Jung jump.

AXIS I: Clinical disorders

Manic-depressive with grandiose delusions (calls himself a Herald to the Grand King) and psychotic features (claims to receive messages from God, talks to self and animals). Suicidal ideation (claims to die with Christ).

Rule out PTSD.

AXIS II: Personality conditions

R/O obsessive-compulsive personality disorder - need to further assess subject's unceasing prayer life and creation of ritualistic practices.

R/O borderline personality disorder – subject appears to have no sense of self, saying he is a living embodiment of the crucified Christ.

AXIS III: Medical conditions

Self-mutilation (subject wears hair shirt; refuses to show stigmata of our Lord, allegedly imprinted on his body; runs into thornbushes; jumps into a pool of ice-cold water).

R/O body dysmorphic disorder – subject calls his body "my brother the ass."

AXIS IV: Psychosocial factors

Embraces poverty (sheds tears of joy over his impoverished state). Need to ascertain if the Order of Friars Minor, the Poor Clares, and the Third Order are officially sanctioned by the Roman Catholic Church or cults.

R/O bestiality.

Poor diet (mixes ashes with food to dilute taste).

When presented with such a case, a treatment plan could include the following: place the subject on suicide watch so he doesn't engage in actions that could lead to martyrdom (only a crazed lunatic would visit the Sultan of Babylon during the Crusades); do a full psychiatric write-up to determine the appropriate drug cocktail; require sessions with a dietician to establish a healthy diet; consult with a medical doctor for appropriate treatment of self-inflicted injuries.

With this kind of a psychosocial history, Francis would never be able to pass the necessary background checks needed to secure a proper church gig.

Paul Moses, author of *The Saint and the Sultan*, gives us a peek into what our world might be like if we put this monk's words into practice. In researching St. Francis's mission to visit the Sultan of Babylon, Moses observed that "the peace Francis spoke of was not the peace of the antiwar movement but something transcendent. It was about creating a new era of reconciliation — in gospel terminology, about creating God's kingdom on earth." Yet if St. Francis came back today, instead of roaming the hills preaching the good news to all, I'm convinced he'd be locked up in a padded cell.

I'm not discounting the good done by psychotropic meds. I've had enough friends with bona fide depressions to know how they were once dead but are now alive thanks to the miracles of modern science.

Yes, I safeguard myself when I'm in the presence of a Times Square preacher who seems more juiced on Jack Daniels than Jesus. My hunch is that most of the time he's spewing Thunderbird, not theology. Then again, if you saw my

> *... crazy like St. Francis, and that's a kind of crazy I'd like to be around.*
> **James Martin**, SJ,
> *My Life with the Saints*

prayer partner Joe, you might think that he's full of something besides the fruit of the Spirit (Galatians 5:22–23). Like me, Joe's definitely an outsider. I'm not sure if he's a saint or not — I'll leave the canonization process up to the pope and his peeps. But Joe gave me some fruit that I definitely needed to eat. A Granny Smith apple never tasted so tart and juicy.

A Prayer Attributed to St. Francis

Lord, make me an instrument of your peace. Where there is hatred, let me sow love; where there is injury, pardon; where there is discord, union; where there is doubt, faith; where there is despair, hope; where there is darkness, light; and where there is sadness, joy.

Grant that I may not so much seek to be consoled as to console; to be understood, as to understand; to be loved, as to love. For it is in giving that we receive, it is in pardoning that we are pardoned, and it is in dying that we are born to eternal life. *Amen.*

Rogue Relative

June 2008

Seems I've always been destined to be a religious satirist. My family first thumbed their noses at the religious powers back in 1620, when my ancestors John Howland, John Alden, and Priscilla Mullins boarded the *Mayflower* in search of the Promised Land. Then in 1630, John Winthrop came to Massachusetts on board the less famous but more politically potent vessel the *Arbella*.

Those on board these two ships shared many of the same theological beliefs (mainly they were both anti-papist to the core and thought the Anglican Church was simply Catholic lite with a British accent). However, the Massachusetts Bay Colony Puritans should not be confused with my *Mayflower* relatives. The *Mayflower* folks, honored once a year in the United States with papier mâché pageants followed by a tryptophan-induced national snooze, were diehard separatists. They wanted nothing whatsoever to do with any state-sanctioned religion. Meanwhile, the Massachusetts crowd showed up with a charter in hand, determined to colonize the country on behalf of King Charles I. They maintained a tenuous connection to the crown and wanted to reform the church without severing their ties to King Charles I, who served as the head of the Church of England.

Governor John Winthrop (1587/8 – 1649) employed biblical language to anoint the Massachusetts Bay Colony as a city upon a hill, a country blessed by God (Matthew 5:14). These Puritans' convictions that their messianic voyage to the New Israel was guided by God were soon challenged by another one of my ancestors. In 1631, the Rev. Roger Williams set sail for the New World in search of

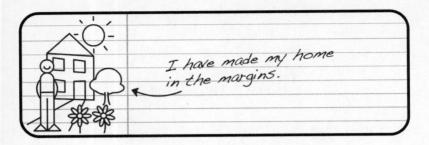

I have made my home in the margins.

religious tolerance. (I can trace my lineage back to Williams's sons Daniel and Joseph. That makes Roger Williams my eleventh and twelfth great-grandfather. Ah, inbreeding. That explains a lot. But I digress.)

As I was growing up, some of my family members pointed out with pride that we were related to a stern-looking statue in downtown Providence, Rhode Island, that was always covered in pigeon poop. Guess that's what you get for founding the smallest state in the Union.

A number of years after my parents' deaths, I felt a tug to explore my family tree. As I detangled these familial roots, I realized even though most Americans might go "Roger who?" the First Amendment bears the imprimatur of my ancestor. When I read on several atheist websites how much they respected this reverend for being a pioneer of religious tolerance, my inner voice told me I might have found one of the keys for opening the door to honest dialogue between thoughtful Christians and atheists.

With all the political bickering leading up to the 2008 election, I decided it was time to reclaim my ancestor's legacy. Admittedly, I'm a satirist and not a scholar. Still, I'm smart enough to realize that one can't simply transfer Williams's pre-Enlightenment ideology to a society that's moved past postmodernism without reducing the endeavor to religious rubbish. Still, maybe he can give me some much-needed perspective as I try to navigate my way through contemporary church-state debates.

I journeyed to Prudence Island, Rhode Island, where my mother's side of the family has vacationed since the turn of the century. According to lore, my ancestor named this idyllic island, as well as neighboring Patience and Hope Islands, after the three virtues he felt everyone should possess — attributes sorely lacking in today's political discourse. No matter what's going on in my life, Narragansett Bay will speak to me, reminding me that this too shall pass.

One day I biked over to Pulpit Rock, where, as legend has it, the Rev. Roger Williams preached to the Narragansett Native Americans. I didn't exactly hear him when I stood at the very spot where he spoke, but the more I read up on Williams, the more I realized we are indeed cut from the same cloth. In addition to being staunch advocates for the separation of church and state, we're up-front, in-your-face people. We're liable to blurt out our opinions, even if it means we're in the definite minority — neither of us being soft-spoken. Williams went so far as to say that forcing one to worship against one's conscience is akin to committing "spiritual soule rape."

Both of us became horrified as kids by what we saw happening in the name of state-sanctioned religion. Growing up in the Bible Belt as an Episcopalian, I've lost count of the number of times I've been told I'm going to hell. As a child, Williams regularly witnessed religious dissenters being burned at the stake near his home in the old Holborn section of London. In reading his accounts, I could have done without all the nasty bloody bits that would have put Stephen King to shame. Pass me the Pepto. But Williams told it like he saw it — blood, guts, and all.

At first, Governor Winthrop welcomed this righteous reverend as a "godly minister." However, before you knew it, these two men were arguing over the same issues that are still being debated today: What role should religion have in society? How do we as a society tolerate people whose beliefs differ from ours? Do dogs go to heaven? You know, the questions that really, really matter.

Seems Winthrop wanted to keep the Massachusetts Bay Colony shining as a Christian "City upon a Hill," a place free from any and all religious dissent. Like any good Puritan, Winthrop wanted to "purify" the church from Anglican excesses, but he wanted to remain in good graces with the crown.

My ancestor took the more radical route, preaching that the church had to make a clean break with the state. He advocated for "soul liberty," a term that I gather means neither the state nor the church can judge the conscience of even the heretic or the atheist. I can't begin to fathom the Christian cojones it took for anyone to stand before the Puritan mob and acknowledge that atheists have a right not to believe in God.

Even though he didn't care for all religions, Williams felt individual conscience must be free from the tyranny of the majority. As he noted, state sponsorship of religion would yield an unhappy situation wherein "the whole world must rule and govern the church." The merger of church and state remains "opposite to the souls of all men who by persecutions are ravished into a dissembled worship which their hearts embrace not."

This is not to say that the righteous reverend felt the state existed in an ethical vacuum. Philosopher Martha Nussbaum observes in *Liberty of Conscience*, "The idea of an overlapping consensus, or, to put it Williams's way, the idea of a moral and natural goodness that we can share while differing on ultimate religious ends, is an idea that helps us think about our common life together much better than the unclear and at times misleading idea of separation." By shifting the focus away from the need to maintain religious orthodoxy to a consensus regarding the "correct belief" on a given issue, we can be free to engage with those who share our common virtues in the hopes of advancing the common good.

However, Williams isn't pulling one of those "anything goes" moves. Just because one can say something doesn't mean he thinks these beliefs shouldn't be held up to scrutiny. If a Christian, say, renounces the resurrection, he should expect other Christians to refute these claims. Furthermore, if a man can't agree with those within a given religious community, then conscience should lead him to separate himself.

These beliefs branded Williams a heretic. Also, his humane treatment of the Native Americans caused quite a stir among the more civilized Englishmen, who viewed Indians as subhuman savages. When he proclaimed that those who originally inhabited this land should be compensated fairly for their property, he became a threat to civilized society.

Things went south for this elder statesman of my family. After a series of escapades running through Salem and Plymouth, Williams got the boot out of godly Massachusetts. He went off into the howling wilderness of winter and settled in Rogues Island (a state that now goes by the more civilized name *Rhode Island*). Here, Williams created a haven for those of any religious persuasion, including those who professed to have no faith. Bill Leonard, dean of Wake Forest Divinity School, observed that "Williams anticipated pluralism, suggesting that non-Christians were effective citizens of the new world."

I ask, whether or no such as may hold forth other worships or religions, Jews, Turks, or anti-Christians, may not be peaceable and quiet subjects, loving and helpful neighbors, fair and just dealers, true and loyal to the civil government? It is clear they may, from all reason and experience in many flourishing cities and kingdoms of the world.

Roger Williams, *The Bloudy Tenent of Persecution for Cause of Conscience*

Also, Williams founded the first Baptist church in America in 1639. (I did not learn this fact until relatively recently because I attended public and Catholic schools where discussions of all things Protestant were strictly prohibited.) But after a couple of months, he left this church and went on to become a seeker of sorts. With so many voices claiming to have the truth, he felt he would have to wait for the new revelation to emerge. In the meantime, he kept looking for evidence of the Spirit wherever he might see it. He remained a Christian, though he never found a church he could call home.

In 1643, Williams set sail for England and began the battle to secure a charter for the state of Rhode Island, thus making liberty of conscience the law of the land. A year later, he published his masterpiece, *The Bloudy Tenent of Persecution for Cause of Conscience*. In this tome, he rants and raves about how ever since

Constantine joined church and state, we've been in the toilet, spiritually speaking.

As expected, Parliament burned and banned his books. Also, Puritan minister John Cotton got his bloomers all in a bunch and wrote a reply titled *The Bloudy Tenent Washed and Made White in the Bloud of the Lambe*. This old stick-in-the-mud toed the party line, arguing that only a fanatic would suggest something as daring as religious liberty. Williams responded with *The Bloudy Tenent Yet More Bloudy: By Mr. Cotton's Endeavor to Wash It White in the Bloud of the Lambe* (1652). Methinks the reverend was giving fellow clergyman Jonathan Swift (1667 – 1745) a run for his money in the religious satire department.

Williams's reputation was further ruined in 1702 when John Cotton's grandson, the Puritan minister Cotton Mather, penned a book that painted him as a dangerous revolutionary. Sounds kind of similar to the hate mail I get some days.

Unfortunately, my ancestor died a loser, shunned by those in proper society as well as by his family and friends. His legacy was partially redeemed in 1777 when William Backus wrote a book that gave him some much-needed props. According to Backus, Williams was a visionary, a man of principle and all that jazz. But Williams's real legacy was secured in 1791, when the Bill of Rights was adopted, including those famous first words of the First Amendment: "Congress shall make no law respecting an establishment of religion, or prohibiting the free exercise thereof." Finally, in 1936, Massachusetts passed a law that rescinded Williams's expulsion from the state.

In spite of the fact that Williams laid the foundation for the First Amendment, politicians these days start humming Winthrop, not Williams, when they want to garner the Christian vote. For reasons that escape me, they trace this phrase's origins to the Founding Fathers instead of giving Williams his props. (They also mistakenly label those who crafted our constitution as Christians when, in fact, they were Deist dudes.)

Also, while select politicos and pundits trot out the "city upon a hill" imagery to bolster their claim that the United States is a Christian nation, they conveniently forget to cite Winthrop's classic "A Model of Christian Charity." If they bothered to reference this document, they'd see how, from the get-go, the United States tried to include at least some provisions to care for those in need. (Though if one was a penniless widow or slave, I doubt they'd use the word *charitable* when describing their treatment at the hands of Colonial-era religious and political leaders.)

The early Puritan Protestant vision of the United States as a redeemer nation and a city upon a hill mythologized into the civic religion of America. This melding of church and state implied that there must be some kind of religious foundation (read: Christianity) in place, so as to perpetuate a select set of values in order to avoid moral chaos.

Williams countered this myth by arguing that forced Christianity is no Christianity at all. He felt men's hearts must remain free to choose their beliefs, adding that if the state privileges Christianity, then it kills the faith. How can anyone accept Christ with free will when these beliefs are force-fed to them by the state? But enough preaching. I wanted to explore more of my ancestor's home turf. Now, if I was a proper historian, I would have ventured into Providence, the city founded by Roger Williams. But to be honest, the sea kept calling my name. So I took off for Newport instead.

Thanks to the kind folks at Go Newport, I played tourist. A quiet

Hey, what's that sound?

159

came over me as I entered Great Friends Meeting House. Built in 1699, this structure was the first church built in Newport. Anne Hutchinson was banished to nearby Portsmouth, though I'm sure she spent some time in prayer and reflection in this simple yet sacred space. Also, while Williams was based in Providence and had an aversion to Quaker meetings, he must have sat still here a time or two.

Even though Newport was founded in 1659 as a colony for religious freedom, this meetinghouse does not stand in the town square. In Newport, unlike nearly every other New England town, there's no shining white church that towers over the other city structures. The lack of a centralized church can be attributed to Rhode Island's passage of the first charter guaranteeing freedom of religion to all faiths. No wonder this city became the home for Touro Synagogue, the oldest synagogue in America. After sailing around the harbor, I spent the rest of my time touring the Newport mansions along Cliff Walk.

Filled with the delight of New England, Williams's wisdom, and a bit of Victorian whimsy, I returned to New York City. On the way home, I began to see my calling in a new light. Speaking my mind and going against the grain is in my genes. But unlike today's political fistfights, Williams and Winthrop disagreed while still remaining friends. (In fact, rumor has it Winthrop warned Williams to flee because Williams was about to be shipped back to England, an act of kindness the good governor had to deny or risk the wrath of King Charles I.)

If Williams and Winthrop can shake hands at the end of the day, what prevents me from extending the hand of compassion and love toward those who drive me nutso? Here's where Christ has to enter the picture, because I can't do this radical-love biz on my own.

While Williams's spirit runs through my veins, I also consider myself a child of God. To be more specific, I'm a practicing Christian who tries to follow the way of Jesus Christ. Despite my brokenness and imperfection, there are moments when I can see the light of Christ trying to shine through (Matthew 5:16). In those brief, fleeting moments, I know I am following not just my eleventh and twelfth great-grandfather but my heavenly Father as well.

When the Saints
Go Marching In

JUNE 28, 2008

When I talk to those outside of the church, I find that we in the church are known more for what we stand against politically than what we stand for spiritually.

Dan Kimball, *They Like Jesus but Not the Church*

In their quest to recast the White House as the Promised Land, both political parties drove their campaign buses into the wall separating church and state during the 2008 presidential election. Rumor has it we live in a pluralistic society, though events ranging from the CNN Compassion Forum to Rick Warren's Saddleback Forum gave the impression we were electing a Christian pastor-in-chief.

When have you all — the respectable leaders — stood up and denounced and called out your haters? You the "moderate" evangelical leaders and "respectable" Republican leadership have nurtured the beast of ignorance in your bosom. Now it's about to bite you — big-time. Your willfully ignorant followers are inflicting the rest of this country with the image of hate, intolerance, and sheer stupidity on a level that is hard to believe.

Frank Schaeffer, author of *Crazy for God*

Back in my twenties, I rebelled against my hippie childhood by aligning myself with organizations such as Young Republicans and Executive Ministries. I bought into the party line that Christians can use their proximity to power and money in the service of enacting God's will here on earth. I've since realized that all too often they end up becoming co-opted into serving the idols of power and money instead.

Even though the 1980s-era Religious Right icons have faded into the sunset, this movement remains embedded at the grassroots level. These Christian cockroaches know how to burrow their way into even the most innocuous-looking church casserole. Through the power of the electronic media, they tug at America's heartstrings like a well-worn country song pining for the return of an imaginary Americana that only exists in TV Land. But check out their flight patterns and funding streams, and it's utterly creepy to see who functions as the wingmen beside these wing nuts.

Take, for example, the "Christian" organization called The Family (or The Fellowship), which hosts the annual National Prayer Breakfast. While all religions are welcome at this event, the underlying message at this ecumenical gathering remains that Jesus is present. However, their version of capitalist Christianity bears no resemblance to the crucified Christ who was sent by God into the world to save the world (John 3:17).

If you will excuse me, I'm going to go look for a more popular kind of Christianity.

©dhayward

Obviously a religious satirist would never be invited to such a high-profile soiree. But from what I've been told, invitations are issued on congressional letterhead and members of the press RSVP through the White

House. Lest anyone feel the Republican party has devolved into a Palinesque parade of lipstick loonies, these elite power brokers operate well under the religious radar, welcoming those Beltway believers who seem all too willing to water down the Beatitudes in the hopes of scoring a seat at this unsacred table.

What kind of political pork could they be serving at this breakfast that would cause religious leaders to get so juiced up on java and Jesus that they forget to follow the First Amendment? While we can long for that promised day described in the book of Revelation when the lion lies down with the lamb, these lions of industry dine on lamb chops. In some progressives' quest to find "common ground," they seem to have fallen into quicksand. That thunderous roar you hear is Roger Williams and the Founding Fathers rolling over in their graves so fast they're liable to cause a nor'easter.

With the Democrats holding the political power (at least for the time being), some religious progressives wanted to get into the game. Organizations such as Clergy for Obama and the Matthew 25 Network (a political action committee that endorsed Obama for president) proved that when fired by their brand of the spirit, progressives can sprint alongside their conservative counterparts.

I'm starting to get a sense of how some conservatives must have felt back in the seventies when people they considered to be their friends began forming what soon became known as the Religious Right. My heart sinks whenever I see religious leaders I respect all decked out in their Obama gear. Just as the GOP doesn't stand for God's Only Party, Jesus did not ride into Jerusalem on a Democratic donkey. When Christians call Jesus of Nazareth "a proponent of 'family values'" or "a community organizer," they've reduced the message of the resurrection to the point where the cross becomes yet another political tool used to solidify a power base.

Religious leaders whose conscience compels them to endorse a particular candidate or party should consider stepping out of the pulpit or a faith-based organization to become a political operative instead. In doing so, they will express their views as an individual voter and not as a representative of the faith.

The anything-goes morality of the religious and political Left is matched by the sanctimonious moralism of the political and religious Right. Uncritical acceptance of any party line is an idolatrous abdication of one's core identity as Abba's child. Neither liberal fairy dust nor conservative hardball addresses human dignity, which is often dressed in rags.

Brennan Manning, *Abba's Child*

Once again, the Holy Spirit has a way of breaking through these man-made political barriers, thus shining forth the power of the risen Christ. Take, for example, the "Jesus for President" tour. In late June, authors and activists Shane Claiborne and Chris Haw, along with the musical renegades the Psalters and other assorted friends, rolled into New York City on their veggie oil–powered bus ready for a new kind of religious revival.

They preached and sang a different tune, proclaiming, "Enough donkeys and elephants. Long live the Lamb." As Shane observed, "This is not about going left or right; this is about going deeper and trying to dream and work together. Rather than endorse candidates, we ask them to endorse what is at the heart of Jesus, and that is the poor and the peacemakers. We are aligned with Jesus and will only get behind those things that move us closer to his upside-down kingdom." Citing examples where both Democrats and Republicans used Jesus as a political pawn to advance their own agendas, the "Jesus for President" crew reminded us that we are electing politicos, not prophets.

Do a president's personal beliefs matter? Yes, I would like for those who govern us to be grounded by some desire to serve the common good. Also, I would hope those in political power have some place where they can go for some minimal self-reflection, whether church, synagogue, mosque, or Walden. In the end, where one chooses to ponder doesn't really matter. After all, President Lyndon B. Johnson, who signed the Civil Rights Act of 1964 into law, became well known for conducting meetings while on the toilet.

Also, according to lore, Martin Luther became inspired by Romans 1:17 ("The righteous will live by faith") while sitting in an outhouse.

Now, should a candidate think he or she has been anointed by God as opposed to being voted in by the electorate and lobbyists, then, Houston, we have a problem. In addition, if they practice a faith like Scientology that requires someone to pray, pay, and obey, then I don't want that person given the keys to the National Treasury. (Along those lines, I want full disclosure for all lobbyists so we know who bought which particular candidate.) Also, when Christians debate the real meaning of the book of Revelation, can they at least come to a consensus that it's not a foreign policy manual?

Whenever I'm asked if I vote, I respond that some women paid such a dear cost for me to have this right that I don't feel I can sit at home on election day. But like Shane, I view voting as "damage control." I go into the voting booth to cast my vote for the candidate I hope will be the more competent person for a particular post. I do not place my ultimate hope in anyone but Christ, for he is the true light I felt shining back in the little town of Bethlehem.

Afterward, Shane asked me what I thought of the message. I told him I loved the irony of bringing an anti-Empire message to New York City, the financial hub of the United States. I prayed that those with ears to hear would let his message sink into their hearts.

The way around the church being a political pawn is by opening ourselves wider to more life experiences with faith in God.

Nathan Diebenow, associate editor,
The Lone Star Iconoclast

Whenever Christians feel seduced into serving an earthly king instead of our King in heaven, perhaps they might want to recall the story of Saul (1 Samuel 9–31). Throughout history, whenever God's people have tried to establish themselves as earthly lords, eventually their kingdom crumbled. Even the best believers can be seduced by the lure of political power, especially if the glare of the media spotlight happens to shine on them. Next thing you know, they end

up advancing their own activist agendas instead of putting the good news into practice.

As inspiring as Shane might be, I'm wondering why those gathered tonight don't reflect the radically inclusive nature of Christ. I gather some homeless guests came to see the show in Philly and a group of homosexuals hosted the "Jesus for President" tour when it came to San Francisco. Here in New York City, the tour is held at Fifth Avenue Presbyterian Church, where barricades have been set up outside in preparation for tomorrow's annual Gay Pride parade. Yet I don't see anyone seated in the pews who will admit to participating in tomorrow's parade or sleeping on the streets. For whatever reason, these "outsiders" weren't invited to join the cool Christian crowd.

For all my talk of equality, I confess I can be classist at times. Left to my own devices, I'll seek out the company of people who share my political and religious beliefs. But while that's comforting, I know it's not Christlike. Maybe I just own the wrong Bible translations, but I can't find any mention of Jesus proclaiming, "I came so that you shall have warm fuzzies."

What keeps us from including the person who isn't perceived

as being part of the "Christian" crowd? Why can't we create space for those who have different religious and political beliefs? Jesus brought together tax collectors, Zealots, and the occasional Jewish religious leader. Heck, he even converted the centurion who stood guard during his crucifixion. If we claim Jesus as our Lord, shouldn't our gatherings accurately reflect the ministry espoused by the radical, rule-breaking, agape-making Jesus? After all, he is our King, and we are his kingdom here on earth. Now that's a Christian conference I'd like to cover.

> *Lord, we are made in your image. Everything we are and have belongs to you. May you always be first in our hearts, in our thoughts, and in our actions. May we follow you in all things, even as we subvert the Empire.*
>
> ***The Missio Dei Breviary***
> (week 4, Monday morning)

Living on a Prayer

July 12, 2008

I'd been in New York City long enough to know that when the temperature rises and you mix men with mullets with Jersey-haired girls, you get a sweaty concoction that smells a bit like Brut and bubble gum. Therefore, when Bon Jovi came to play in Central Park, I decided not to reach out and touch someone. But I wanted to participate in this Manhattan happening, so I picked the one spot near the park I suspected this crew wouldn't hit — the rooftop garden of the Metropolitan Museum of Art.

Bingo. The artsy crowd mingled among Jeff Koons's larger-than-life whimsical sculptures, oblivious to the Bridge & Tunnel brigade building beneath them. I said a quick prayer of thanks that I was up here instead of down there. I circled *Balloon Dog (Yellow)*, a Koons' creation that looked like some gigantic superhero's pet. The setting sun's reflection danced around the sculpture and me as though we were playing keep-away.

The primal beats of guitars and drums signaled that Bon Jovi was in the house. The music kept building until even the most refined art aficionado hummed along. The moment Bon Jovi blasted out "Livin' on a Prayer," I was looking up *Balloon Dog (Yellow)*'s behind. I freely admit that staring at a balloon dog's rear end isn't quite the same thing as adoring a religious icon. But at that moment, this whimsical sculpture somehow drew me in, and I began to hear this eighties rock anthem in a new light. Draw your own connection between Koons and Christ; I just wanted to savor this moment. When I was a kid, my family seldom frequented museums, took in a play, attended a classical concert, or even saw a film with subtitles (Japanese horror movies don't count). Hence, I didn't grow up with a genuine appreciation for the arts.

So in college I was fair game for those academic anarchists who sneered at this Southern blonde preppy who dared to enter their conformist creative circles.

"Who told her she had any talent?"

"We don't do debutantes."

"Stick to your pearls, sweetie."

To this day I have no clue why I stuck it out when everyone in the theatre department kept telling me to scram. But I kept feeling there was something inside of me that had to burst out or I'd implode. My family labeled me the "dreamer," as though that meant I had some kind of mental defect when, in fact, I was just "different."

I wandered around in no-man's-land, wanting to express myself, yet fearful that whatever I might create would get trashed and trampled. Whenever I would try to offer any kind of a creative contribution, those pseudo-intellectuals looked at me askance, as though I were somehow stinking up their saintly sanctuary. (Sometimes the line blurs between clergy and critics.)

In the documentary *Before the Music Dies*, soul singer and song-

> *The pain of making the necessary sacrifices always hurts more than you think it's going to. I know. It sucks. That being said, doing something seriously creative is one of the most amazing experiences one can have, in this or any other lifetime. If you can pull it off, it's worth it. Even if you don't end up pulling it off, you'll learn many incredible, magical, valuable things. It's not doing it when you know full well you had the opportunity — that hurts far more than any failure.*
> **Hugh MacLeod,** *Ignore Everybody*

writer Erykah Badu made some astute observations about the music industry that can be applied to any creative enterprise. She noted there are three kinds of artists: (1) those who hurt to do what they do; (2) the one who imitates those in pain (these are often the rich ones); and (3) those who do what somebody tells them to do.

I definitely fall into the first category. A friend once told me, "Becky, you make people very uncomfortable because you remind them of the pain they've been trying to hide." I applaud those who can put up with me when I open up my guts and give birth to a book. In the process, a few people I thought were friends and fellow travelers bolt and head for the hills.

At times I wish I could join them. Seems I can never unpack my personal baggage without having my junk strewn all over the place. What some call "passion" others dismiss as "pain in the rear end." More often than I care to admit, I end up throwing a full-blown Calvin-styled temper tantrum when I should be demonstrating more Hobbeslike wisdom and restraint. (Where is cartoonist Bill Watterson when we need him?)

Also, my suitcase never seems to close properly, so I can't stuff myself back in, all neat and tidy, and simply move on to the next adventure. I'm the one walking around the hallowed halls of Christendom with theological toilet paper stuck to my shoe. During these moments when I feel like some dog in desperate need of a flea bath, I take comfort in Mike Yaconelli's messiness — for he seemed to have a similar packing problem.

On a whim, I took a class at Yale Divinity School in which we acted out Bible stories. (I have no clue why I signed up for this, but my gut told me I had to do it.) Our final project was a performance of the Bible. I remember leaving some classes in tears over the taunting a few students gave me when the teacher wasn't looking.

"You really lack any stage presence and rhythm whatsoever."

"Let me show you how it's done."

"Maybe you should visit the writing tutor."

Fortunately, Professor Peter Hawkins was in charge of casting the show. He assigned two roles to me — Isaac, the sacrificial son, and a grandmother who tells the story of her two prodigal grandchildren.

When I performed those pieces, somehow I was able to silence the spiritual snots and simply inhabit the roles. For a brief period of time, I connected not with the words I was saying but with the souls of the characters. Afterward, a few people came up to me almost in tears. I just stood there, wondering what the heck happened that night. But the spark to write that had been brewing inside me began to smolder.

The embers didn't catch fire until a few years later when Mike Yaconelli and Robert Darden took me under their wings and opened *The Wittenburg Door* for me. Somehow, they saw my light during that period when I groped around in the dark. Mix together my constant cravings to put pen to paper with my disgust for undivine dorks — and thus marks the unexpected birth of a religious satirist.

A similar dynamic happened again in 1996, when I connected with my improv teacher, Gary Austin, and his wife, Wenndy MacKenzie, who later became my vocal coach. They taught me how to get out of my head and into my heart. By not thinking about what I want to do but simply responding to what's happening around me, I can get in touch with the essence of who I am — junk and all. When I'm in this frame of mind, I try to silence both my inner critic that tries to get me to "behave" and those professional critics who try to inform me as to what I "ought to appreciate."

Sometimes, when I'm at a religious retreat, everyone else seems to be meditating on a piece of art, a poem, or something else that's supposedly charged with meaning. Meanwhile, I'm sitting there looking like a devotional deer in the holy headlights. During the Everything Must Change tour, Linnea Capshaw did an amazing presentation using an abstract art exhibit titled *Nude Truths: An Odyssey in Poetry, Painting, and Prose*. I wanted to be moved. But when I went to write, nothing came out. It wasn't writer's block; it was simply that I didn't connect — unlike some others, who wrote poetry responses that really spoke from their hearts. Instead of ascribing blame when I don't "get it," I've learned to just let go. Not every moment can be magical.

The key for me remains finding what works and then following that path. One of my prized discoveries is the Met's Robert

Lehman Collection. In this quiet spot of paradise, I can soak in Christ to Cézanne sans the onslaught of tourists talking. They gravitate toward the "must-see" sights such as Impressionists, the Temple of Dendur, and the Costume Institute. Sometimes this place is so quiet I feel like I've been cast as the child in *The Nutcracker*. The old masters dance off the canvas to host an *Alice in Wonderland*–themed party. We raise our seventeenth-century goblets and toast Botticelli's *The Annunciation*. Even Van Gogh smiles.

To get to this collection, I have to walk past the Mary and Michael Jaharis Galleries for Byzantine Art and the Medieval Europe Gallery. The soft lighting and plethora of stained glass and crosses make it feel so much like a church that whenever I enter this space, I almost cross myself. In these medieval masterpieces, Jesus almost seems to be "enjoying" the crucifixion, as though he's already heaven bound even while the Good Friday massacre unfolds here on earth.

My favorite part of this collection remains the reliquaries — a collection of bones, body parts, and other saintly treasures. When I get into a real medieval mind-set, I venture up to The Cloisters, where their collection also includes tomb effigies, sepulchral monuments, and gothic gardens. For a brief period, a traveling exhibit from the Victoria and Albert Museum featured the reliquary of St. Thomas Becket. Ah, so that's where his  bones went (or so they say). A side of me wanted to take a peek, but Becket's bits remained under lock and key. I guess that's all for the best. This pilgrim isn't up for another chilling Canterbury experience. Ni, ni, ni.

The challenge remains to deepen my appreciation and critical eye without taking myself too seriously and thus losing the child-like wonder. I don't like it when my critical voice yells at my inner child. After all, a museum, a film festival, a stage, or even a church should always be a place to play and praise — a home for everyone, including misfits like me.

> *you don't fit and that's your gift... if somebody is asking a lot of questions, doesn't fit, is creative — don't push them away. give them the space to create something different and new and resist the temptation to co-opt it.*
>
> **Jonny Baker**

The Ordinary Radicals

> *Nobody in his or her right mind would want to be a member of a socially acceptable religion. It's very dangerous for the soul.*
>
> **Phyllis Tickle,** interview in *The Wittenburg Door*

Jamie Moffett, cofounder of The Simple Way, calls himself an ex-Christian, but he doesn't paint all believers with the same blasphemous brush. He produced and directed *The Ordinary Radicals* because he wanted to break the stereotypes surrounding the faith that he used to follow. In this documentary, he shines a light on those who seek to do "small things with great love."

As one of the many folks interviewed for this flick, I wanted to support this Moffett mania. On a hotter-than-Hades September day, I set out for Philadelphia to attend this film's premiere. To add to the heat, my scheduled train from Trenton to Philly got canceled when a branch fell on top of the train. Maintaining one's sense of Christian character can be quite dicey when one is surrounded by pounding iPods, businessmen with BO, cranky children, and other urban delights. Somehow, I managed to arrive at the theatre without blowing an ungodly gasket.

I was honored to be in this film and delighted when my snarky on-screen self got one of the biggest laughs of the evening. But I was also relieved that I said my bit and moved on, so that the ordinary radicals could get their turn to shine. While this film definitely highlights many underground activists, a few friends reminded me that there's nothing ordinary about many of those in the film. Yes, many of us live in various states of volunteer poverty. But hardly any writers get the opportunity to have their works published, let along get speaking invites, publisher-paid author tours, and other perks that some authors/speakers seem to take for granted.

Alas, seeing a few people hog the limelight did bring out the jealous streak in me. Anne Lamott reflects, "Jealousy is one of the occupational hazards of being a writer, and the most degrading. And I, who have been the Leona Helmsley of jealousy, have come to believe that the only things that help ease or transform it are (a) getting older, (b) talking about it until the fever breaks, and (c) using it as material." I usually end up with option (b), though in lieu of conversation, I'm liable to throw an unholy hissy fit.

After I cooled down a bit, I realized I was being a modern-day Jonah who was having another Nineveh moment (Jonah 4). After all, this wasn't about me but the ordinary radicals.

Yes, this documentary demonstrated that Christians don't speak with one voice, though clearly much more needs to be done. Here's praying that those of us (myself definitely included) who have the mic will pass it on. Some days, Wormwood from *The Screwtape Letters* catches me on a bad day, and I allow him to massage my ego by trying to convince me of my own self-importance.

Admittedly, giving up the spotlight represents a hurdle that I find challenging. Sometimes when I recommend a fellow writer, I can hear Wormwood whispering to me in the background.

"Once they get into a position of influence, they'll outshine you."

The next step, rather than being a voice for the "voiceless," is to hand the mic over to indigenous community leaders and ask them to facilitate the conversation so that we might grow and deepen in relationship with one another and with God.

Jason and Vonetta Storbakken, "Reconciliation's Challenge for New Monastic Communities"

You bet it hurts like heck when I open the door only to have it slammed in my face every so often. Still, I know in my heart that the only way moving forward is to keep encouraging new voices, trusting that all of our voices matter. In the end, what's the point of having street cred if you don't use it to build up the neighborhood? As a writer, my job is to just try to get the conversation started.

Go West, Young Man

SEPTEMBER 2008

With this open-mic mind-set, I set out for the Pacific Northwest. Finally, after considerable online exchanges, I got to connect in real time with the Revs. Karen Ward and Kurt Neilson, as well as hang out a bit with Bill Dahl from *The Porpoise Diving Life*.

First stop — Seattle. Karen, the abbess for Church of the Apostles (COTA), gave me a quickie tour of the funky Fremont section of Seattle, including the infamous troll and Lenin statues. I had heard so many mountaintop experiences of people who have visited this Anglican-Lutheran church plant that I had built a montage in my mind of what I thought this trip should be like. But it all seemed so ordinary. In my constant New York state of mind, I tended to perceive ordinariness to be mundane and frankly boring. After dinner, I settled into one of COTA's three hermitages, tired and, to be honest, a bit disillusioned. This is it?

I spent my days writing in coffee shops (this is Seattle, after all), visiting a few other friends, and playing tourist. Over lunch and a walk around Green Lake, Eliacín Rosario-Cruz from the Mustard Seed Associates and I talked about the simple ways that Mustard Seed works within the community. We also touched a bit on the sticky issue of race and New Monasticism®, and I applauded the way he tries to make his presence known as a Puerto Rican working within a largely Anglo culture.

Gary Austin, one of the kindest souls on the planet, connected me with a character in Seattle named Don Goldberg. He attends a synagogue that's not a synagogue and would consider himself to be mystical and spiritual but not religious. So I thought he was a good soul to chat with about spirituality, Seattle style. While considerable ink has been spilled discussing the variants between denominations and their accompanying theologies, too little attention has been paid to how a region's history and local issues often inform one's spiritual perspective.

Don explained that Seattle is one of the most literate places in North America, adding that people who develop critical thinking skills don't like to be told how to think. Like the Native Americans who settled this place, Seattle residents have a spiritual sense. They don't necessarily go to a church, but they're in a place with incredible natural beauty. So, according to Don, they resist hearing from someone who's going to quote Scripture and tell them a set of rules they have to follow in order to achieve what they already know is readily available. Also, he reminded me that Seattle remained isolated from the rest of the country for years, free to develop its own craziness and cults without much scrutiny.

As the week progressed, I got in sync with the everyday rhythm of COTA. No mountaintop moments — I'm in Seattle, not Sinai. But the mellow vibe makes even this overactive New Yorker start napping for the first time in years.

COTA's Benedictine simple hospitality brought to mind my experiences visiting mayBe and Grace in the UK this past summer. No wonder church leaders from around the world journey to COTA for a learning pilgrimage. I'm joined this week by a few Brits — a couple from Home, an Oxford-based faith community, and the Rev. Paul Roberts, the founder of Foundation, a community in Bristol.

You seldom find Karen up front and center, though her faith fingerprints can be seen all over COTA. As Karen recounted her story, I learned that COTA was a dream that was fueled partly by the Call to Common Mission, a joint Lutheran-Episcopal full communion agreement. Under Karen's quiet leadership, six people met for Bible study and prayer to explore what kind of a community they wanted to create. From these seeds, a full-fledged congregation came to fruition.

On first glance, some might dismiss some of these fruits as being too exotic and unique. They don't fit in with the prepackaged ingredients that make up the watered-down ambrosia served at church potlucks. Often they're treated like weeds that need to be pruned in order to create "pretty church." But under Karen's watchful eye, she's nurtured a group of gardeners who have created this somewhat unruly yet healing garden where I could really rest (Matthew 11:28).

There is no quick fix, no silver bullet, no magic pill that can create community or help people want to share their faith. We can only turn to God and ask to be used for God's purposes. When people do that for real — individually and in small groups in a congregation — miracles begin to emerge.

Martha Grace Reese, author
of the Unbinding the Gospel series

When church planters inquire about COTA, Karen finds they're often looking for some emergent elixir that will somehow magically re-tradition their beige and boring worship service into a rockin' religious rainbow. But there is no secret to COTA's success. When people call her up and ask, "What do you do?" the question perplexes her. "We're a church. What do people think we do? We do what every church does — we celebrate Communion, we perform the other sacraments such as baptisms, confirmations, and marriages. We counsel the brokenhearted, admonish the wayward, and engage in other pastoral activities you'd expect from a church. Just because we don't look like a church doesn't mean we aren't one."

Even though Karen doesn't like to be collared (she seldom wears clerical gear), that doesn't mean she's not centered. She didn't just slap some logos on her blog and call herself a church planter. Rather, Karen went through the steps to become a Lutheran pastor, though she has now been received as an Episcopal priest. When asked by a member of the Commission on Ministry what she brings to the Episcopal Church, she replied, "Trouble." To those who question why anyone would want to muddy up the Episcopal waters even more, Karen's brand of "trouble" differs vastly from the Anglican antics currently on display. As she observes, "God troubled the waters at creation. When things get stagnant, there's lifelessness. So I stir things up in hopefully a good way."

The COTA community transformed the dilapidated and abandoned Fremont Abbey into an arts center with central multiuse space. This work in progress glows with warm welcome, giving off a homey burnt yellow glow. As part of their goal to make the Abbey self-sufficient, through the Fremont Abbey Arts Center, they rent out space to activities as diverse as the Fremont Music School, contra dance classes, and an eco-fashion show. I took in a bit of Round 40, an underground folk music and poetry slam that had Seattle written all over it. Unfortunately, I missed the monthly Goth mass and the biweekly theology pub, though I was able to join Hysteria, the weekly women's group, for an evening of chatting and knitting.

During my stay in Seattle, I felt blessed to celebrate COTA's third confirmation. Karen put on her clerical "costume" at the request of the six confirmands, who wore their black baptismal shirts. As the curator, Karen oversaw the service, though the most active person during the service is the musical director, Lacey Brown. The bulk of the congregants represent twentysomething burned-out evangelicals, though I did spot some people in the over-forty category.

Bishop Greg Rickel reflected in his sermon on how one of his Lambeth 2008 highlights was hearing Brian McLaren single out Karen Ward and COTA as an example of innovative, emerging Anglicanism. Karen sank back a bit as though she wished to shine the attention on COTA instead of herself. I admire her humble soul, though I keep encouraging her to tell her story. She represents one of the many invisible voices that tend to get drowned out by the constant yammering of those postmodern pseudo-prophets who market themselves as relevant, relational, and real. We can't say we're truly the church of the future if we keep on singing the same old songs led by the usual suspects.

During portions of the service, hymns and lessons were projected on the wall, while a translucent image of Jesus emerged and then faded into the background. This thin-line imagery, where I felt Jesus' presence without seeing his face, transported me back to the Irish soil I visited for the first time last summer. Once again, I didn't need to speak Jesus' name, but his presence spoke loud and clear. In fact, one can find more Scripture woven into  the fabric of an Anglican liturgy than at many nonliturgical church services. (So none of this "Anglicans aren't biblical" biz or I'll sic a sacristan on you.) Following the sermon, a time of quiet called "Open Space" presented us with the opportunity to reflect via several interactive prayer stations, or we could simply stay and meditate in our seats.

Mars Hill Mania

No religious satirist's trip to Seattle could be considered complete without seeing the Mark Driscoll Show. After all, Mars Hill Church is rumored to be the missional monster, the Godly Godzilla, that invaded the Seattle area with more than seven campuses.

Despite Seattle's secular status, the Ballard Campus, where Mark speaks up close and personal, averages close to four thousand attendees each week, with sermons fed into the other campuses. (Apparently plans are under way to plant a hundred global campuses.) Additional stats, such as the 4.4 million sermon downloads

from the church's website and the eight hundred church planters trained internationally during the past year, demonstrate that this is indeed an evangelical empire.

Prior to the service, I wondered if I could stomach his stuff. I've lost track of the number of times someone sent me a YouTube video of Mark Driscoll spewing proclamations that made my ears bleed. Still, I felt I had an obligation to move beyond Mark's machismo to see what's attracting these eager evangelicals. I managed to cover Joel Osteen, Creflo Dollar, and Fred Price for *The Wittenburg Door* without losing my mind, my mission, or my meal, so I figured I could take whatever Driscoll dished out.

I almost missed Mars Hill Church's Ballard Campus because I thought this black-and-gray building was a low-rent community college. After I walked by the information booth and small gift stand, I crossed into the auditorium and was handed a program. According to my bulletin, the church had loads of fellowship groups and redemption groups to help the fallen pray away their sins. But what about those who come to church hungry and homeless? How come a church this large doesn't even have a drop-in center of sorts for those in need that can provide at least something to eat and maybe a warm place to rest?

A holier-than-thou version of Avril Lavigne blasts out power pop tunes accompanied by the all-white coed praise band Sons of Thunder. Not-so-funky graphics played on the projector. A wooden cross on the stage almost faded into the beige background.

No latte-loving losers in this house. No siree. Mark Driscoll embodies the revitalization of muscular Christianity. This Victorian-era movement began as a revolt against women-led church that made men soft and continues today through groups like Promise Keepers. With an emphasis on building up one's body and soul, these men bond together like some kind of spiritual superglue. The women stand off to the side, willing and ready to serve.

Once the crowd got pumped up and primed to praise, the graphic logo "Pray like Jesus" sizzled on the screen. Time for the Biblical BBQ!

Mark Driscoll entered front and center, looking slightly scruffy yet totally relevant in his untucked shirt and jeans with a Bible propped in his hand, puppet style. He's more wired than I am. But while he doesn't have that laid-back Seattle vibe, I'm not seeing the theological testosterone he displays in his YouTube clips.

His sermon taught us how to pray like Jesus, Gethsemane style: pray for self, the disciples, and the church. Mark rattled off a whole list of sexual sins that require major prayer — sex before marriage, same-sex marriage, divorce. (You know, the evangelical big no-no's.)

I waited for the real juicy bits where Mark goes on about how he doesn't respect any pastor he can beat up or how he blames pastors' wives when their husbands stray because they let themselves go. Instead, he put on his mellow Mark mask, reflecting that "when we talk with other Christians, we need to be gracious, humble, loving. Don't be deceived. Debate, not division."

What the?!? I'm not going to witness any of his controversial unchristian crapola? C'mon. The very least the cussing pastor can do is cut loose with a couple of swearwords.

As quickly as he entered, Mark exited. For all his talk about prayer, he never engaged in said act with his congregation. Heck, they didn't have any prayers of the people or any other kind of corporate prayer.

Next, an assistant pastor encouraged us to come forward for Communion. Despite Mars Hill Church's conservative stances, they got a bit progressive by offering grape juice and wine. Also, we were served Communion by male and female ushers — nice to see the girls get to do more in Mark Land than minister to their men and clean up poop in the nursery. Still, no one offered any words of institution or even a few words of Scripture, and I wondered how many people connected what they received with the Last Supper (Matthew 26:17 – 30; Mark 14:12 – 25; Luke 22:7 – 20).

Yet another pastor came out and gave us some final instructions. He encouraged us to get involved in The City, Mars Hill Church's online network. Those who were church members were encouraged to make their usual offering, but visitors like me weren't pressured into giving. Also, pastors were at the front of the church after the service so one could get a piece of prayer if need be.

After we were dismissed, I walked out into the lobby in search of signs of Driscoll. No pastors were present, though I did see several guys with earpieces and black "Mars Hill Security" T-shirts. What's with the biblical bouncers? Let's be honest. The "limp-wristed hippies" Driscoll slams might be full of hot air, but I seriously doubt any of them pack heat.

Believe it or not, I get the appeal of this place. In today's troubled times, Driscoll presents black-and-white answers to a world cloaked in gray. On one level he's right. Too many socially conscious progressives lack a biblical backbone. For all their talk about global and corporate sin, they never address the personal challenges in trying to actually follow Jesus (Matthew 8:18–22).

Also, I've walked into more than my share of churches where I felt people welcomed my cash but didn't want to care about me. For those who feel lonely and disconnected, Mars Hill Church offers a cup of lukewarm coffee and ready-made community with no immediate pressure to pledge. Even lousy coffee and a warm handshake could warm one up a little bit.

When I first graduated from college, I sought out churches that were social hubs for singles. If Mars Hill Church had been around back then, I might have given this place a shot. But I doubt this community would have worked for me because I was never "saved" enough to interest those men looking for a Suitable Helper or a True Christian™ woman.

Also, I'm at a point in my life where I need a bit more Christ caring and much less God swearing. I can list my sins alphabetically or chronologically, depending on one's personal preference. So telling me that I'm a you-know-what only confirms what I already know. What I seek out are places where I can find rest in God's grace, surrounded by other broken believers.

After the Mars Hill Experience, I reconnected with Karen Ward and Paul Roberts for Compline at Saint Mark's Episcopal

Cathedral. Young adults filled the space, though, as Karen noted, these kids see Sunday night at the Cathedral to be more of a cool date night than a religious experience. They don't get connected to the church — unless, of course, they meet Karen. She won't try to "save" anyone; that's not her style. But after you've spent a bit of time in her presence, you'll want to hang out in her English garden and sample whatever she's drinking, whether it's Belgian beer or the Bible.

Redmond Revelations

I could have stayed and soaked up Seattle, but Bill Dahl, a "gruff around the edges" Santa Claus kind of guy, planned plenty of action in Redmond, Oregon. So off I went via Amtrak and the Central Oregon Breeze bus.

Bill arranged for a few events that took the form of spiritual salons of sorts. Instead of one person being front and center lecturing and leading, the goal was to give those present a chance to dialogue and interact — attributes sorely lacking in most typical author monologues. At times I dominated the discussion (again), so not everyone may have left feeling they were heard or had contributed to the conversation. I talk about opening the door to all, but too often I don't practice what I preach.

This local and relational way of gathering seems to be catching on as the way to move the dialogue forward. On his blog, Andrew Jones reflects, "Let's move away from celebrity-based speaker-fests toward something that is relational, communal, sustainable, accessible, and worthwhile. Using homes, kitchens, couches, campgrounds may sound terribly invasive to some who would rather pop into a Sheraton and go home again, but a conference should be an opportunity to experience church on a deep level."

At first glance, this contemporary holy hippie may come off as a bit too granola and generous — preaching peace and passing out daisies. But hang around this Tall Skinny Kiwi for a while, and you'll realize he might look like a Jesus freak but he's definitely not stuck in the sixties. Instead, he's on the road trying to tune in to the frequency of where God might be calling him.

In my research into how to build grassroots ministries that are sustainable and Christ centered, I've gleaned practical wisdom from Shannon Hopkins, a UK-based missional entrepreneur and a U.S. emerging church pioneer. When she was asked, "With all the needs out there, how do you set priorities or determine where God is calling you?" Shannon wrote this thoughtful response:

> To be honest, there is no set formula; however, some of the elements are always the same (kind of like when you go to bake a cake, and you always have sugar, butter, and flour).
>
> For me, part of the formula, obviously, comes through prayer and discernment, and part of it is based on the people God brings me into relationship with (I find the best way to engage in relational discipleship is by working on things with people). Part of it is promptings and passions (what God is putting on my heart at the moment), and part of it is an awareness of where culture is at or where it is heading....
>
> My work is missional at the core, and I am looking for ways to bring transformation both to individuals, communities, and the culture at large. So that also provides a filter. It allows me to ask the questions: Will people experience the kingdom of God through this project? Will people see Jesus in this work?

Throughout my travels, I'm starting to sense how many people possess this inner longing to connect with Jesus. I've even heard a few stories about some post-Christian a/theist types meeting to talk about Jesus. Even in the absence of a formal religion, the cravings continue.

These folks tend to be classified by pollsters as "dechurched" or "unchurched." Such terms bring to mind such unpleasant imagery as "deloused" and "unwashed" — the implication being that those who choose not to be passive pew sitters are somehow unclean. In fact, those sitting stone-silent in the sanctuary may be the ones who need to be saved from themselves. I coined the phrase "those for whom *church* is not in their vocabulary" because it struck me as a neutral way to describe those who don't "do church."

I believe God is inviting us to move out beyond the confines of the safe harbors named when (Sunday), what (spiritual entertainment), why (tradition, routine, guilt or ritual), how (sermons and songs) and where (church) we have come to expect to find him.

Bill Dahl, *The Porpoise Diving Life*

During our downtime in Redmond, Bill and I took a walk along the Metolius River, located outside Sisters, Oregon. Bill shared with me his peace-creation mission in Redmond. Every year, the Dahls take in one or two Muslim boys as part of a student exchange program without any preconceived agenda. In this process, they have witnessed a myriad of myths melt in their living room as they shared their daily life together. By opening up their home and their lives to "the other," new dimensions of Christ are revealed to them.

The Dahls chose to take in Muslim students because the numbers of Muslim students desiring to experience an international exchange year in the United States dropped off dramatically after the 9/11 terrorist attacks. Bill reflected how high school–age Muslims have become the innocent victims of vicious stereotypes, adding that they make tremendous contributions in championing cultural diversity at Redmond's local high school.

Since Muslims have large extended families scattered in other countries, these connections that begin in Redmond spread around the world. When I was sitting with religious and political leaders in Amman talking about ways to encourage American-Jordanian dialogue, I could not imagine I would hear similar sentiments expressed in conservative central Oregon. If these cross-cultural exchanges can happen in Bill's living room, what prevents us from trying similar measures elsewhere?

I found a glimmer of hope when I caught a screening of the documentary *Pray the Devil Back to Hell*. This film tells the compelling story of how Christian and Muslim women of Liberia joined forces to combat the violent warlords and the corrupt regime of Charles Taylor. During the press conference held during the 2008 Tribeca

Film Festival, I learned from Leymah Gbowee, the leader of this movement, that Roman Catholic archbishop and former president of the Liberian Council of Churches Michael K. Francis became her spiritual rock. The behind-the-scenes prophetic presence of Francis and other religious leaders gave these women the faith fuel they needed to keep on marching.

Armed with white T-shirts, the power of prayer, and their Bibles or Qur'ans, these women won a long-awaited peace that led to the election of Ellen Johnson Sirleaf, Africa's first elected female head of state. In one scene that had the audience cheering, these women barricaded the site of the stalled peace talks in Ghana. The men could not leave the room, even to eat, until they drafted a workable peace plan. When the guards tried to arrest the women, they employed the most powerful nonviolent weapon in their arsenal by threatening to remove their clothes. This strategy worked, as the guards chose not to bring shame on themselves by forcing the women to expose their naked bodies. The women kept their clothes on, and they kept their promise to pray and work for peace.

While I knew bits about Bill from his Porpoise Diving Life website, I see now there's much more to this underground activist than what one might glean by reading his insightful, and at times off-the-wall, ramblings.

Leaders should be manure.

Followers should bloom.

Seattle Redux

Onward to Portland. Time to hang with Karen Ward's partner in Christian crime, the Rev. Kurt Neilson of Saints Peter and Paul Episcopal Church. Kurt gave me a tour of this urban church, pointing out the St. Brigid's cross and other visible reminders of the Celtic spirituality he encountered during his pilgrimages to Ireland and Iona. He had a labyrinth designed on the lawn of this urban parish. For those not familiar with this ancient meditative practice, Mark Pierson, worship curator and pastor, describes a labyrinth as a winding path — a bit like a maze, but with just one path so you can't get lost. He says, "People used to walk the path of the labyrinth as a form of pilgrimage; winding their way into the centre and then out again. Many experienced it as a journey toward the divine, at the centre of the labyrinth, and back out into the world."

The labyrinths I see in cathedrals tend to be roped off, so I could look but not touch this ancient spiritual practice. But once I traced my steps around a stone labyrinth at the Cliff House in Ogunquit, Maine, I felt my body calming down in a way that I hadn't been able to achieve through other meditative practices. Since then, whenever I see a labyrinth, I try to check it out. As much as I would have liked to walk this particular urban maze, that wasn't a viable option. A local with a drinking problem tried to thank the church for its kindness by cleaning up the weeds around this sacred spot. In his inebriated state, he mowed down the labyrinth.

After a vandal stenciled the words *welcome slave* and a motif of Jesus, the church responded to this act by whitewashing out the word *slave* and letting the welcome stand.

I oriented myself in Oregon the same way I did in Seattle: I found a welcoming coffee shop with Wi-Fi. I nestled myself next to the cardboard cutouts of Barack Obama and John McCain at the Bipartisan Café and hunkered down to work. This allegedly bipartisan coffeehouse exposed their blue-state bias, as they served up a bold Obama blend from Kenya, whereas the milder McCain blend hailed from Panama.

A Celtic ethos permeates the church's mission and ministry, with the Columba Center forming the centerpiece of the church's work in the world. By following a rule of life, these largely lay monastics put into practice the notion of "thin space." I encounter this porous border between this world and the next when I touch God's creation through fly-fishing, kayaking, or hiking. Hence, I've always considered that connecting with thin space involved some type of an outdoor adventure. Yet this urban community found this permeable border hidden beneath the concrete and grit of East Portland. This got me thinking: Where else have I overlooked this Celtic connection?

The church's ministries, Brigid's Table and Rahab's Sisters, put into practice the question posed by the scribe in the story of the good Samaritan, "Who is my neighbor?" (Luke 10:29), and the message of radical welcome found in Hebrews, "Do not forget to show hospitality to strangers, for by so doing some people have shown hospitality to angels without knowing it" (Hebrews 13:2).

Kurt arranged for me to assist with serving at Brigid's Table, a weekly sit-down meal for the homeless. Here the delineation between volunteer and homeless became obliterated. For that brief evening, we were fellow companions in the journey, sharing a meal together. This past year, I had a financial crisis that almost did me in. Had it not been for those around me, I could have ended up at a place like Brigid's Table, not as a server, but as a guest.

"This is the only place I can go where I'm treated like a human being."

"You're the one church in town that lets people come in even if they've been drinking. I like that."

"I don't have to sing for my supper. I hate those song and sandwich churches. But I gotta eat."

"I decided to clean up the day after my dog died. She didn't do anything wrong. But I couldn't find any money to take care of her when she got sick. I walked all over and over. No one would give me any money to take her to the hospital. She was just a little dog. I held her close to me that night, hoping my body would keep her warm. I went to sleep. I woke up. She didn't. I killed the only thing that still loved me. That's when I realized I had to do something. It's not easy, but I'm trying."

Looks to me like they're serving a lot more than just Vegetable Lo Mein and egg rolls with brownies for dessert. I've covered many faith-based feeding programs, but I can't remember the last time I saw one filled with this much love. Social service programs may feed people, but how many of them provide the bread of life? Perhaps some of the soil I walked on at Glendalough and Kildare got transplanted back here somehow. It sure feels like it.

On Friday night, I assisted Rahab's Sisters with their ministry of presence to Portland's prostitutes. In addition to a few members of Saints Peter and Paul Church, I met some women from Imago Dei, several women from other Episcopal congregations, and a few volunteers whose affiliations escaped me. As much as the guests appreciated the food, toiletries, and clean underwear, what seemed to matter most was that for one night a week, they could sit down in a safe place where they wouldn't be judged.

These women reminded me of my mother during the last years of her life. Once beaming and full of life, she reached a point where she was too tired to survive. This ministry infused these women with the hope to hang on. I wonder what might have happened if my mother had found a group like Rahab's Sisters during her downward spiral.

Afterward, I set out for Casa Jessie, home of the church's resident hospitality queen, who hosts many of the church's visitors. Just as I was about to cross the street, a group of teens from Victory Outreach International Twilight Treasures Ministry Jesus-jumped me. They were so on fire for the Lord and sure of their salvation that they could only hear their own voices. Normally I blow off street evangelists because they give me the creeps in a clownlike kind of way. But they looked so happy-holy that I let them thrust their love offering into my hand. We Bible-blessed each other, and I left. But

193

I didn't need their tracts, for I had seen the invisible hand of God in action.

My online buddy Rosalie Grafe and I finally connected face-to-face. Her spiritual journey illustrated how one person can carve out a niche ministry. After her divorce, she joined the community of Northumbria, which provided her with the spiritual grounding to inform her daily life and work. In the Benedictine tradition of hospitality, she set up Quaker Abbey, where she sees herself as a soul friend to fellow wandering pilgrims. Also, Quaker Abbey Press enables her to do very small print runs of books so she can give a voice to those writers whose work she wants to illuminate.

She has defined her ministry as a "butt in the chair" presence — the person in the background who shows up so the youth group has enough chaperones, who visits the man in prison that no one wants to see anymore, and who does other small acts of kindness that are often noticed only by God. I began reflecting on how many Rosalies I've met who smiled at me when I thought I was going to lose it. How do we encourage and nurture these everyday saints? I seldom know their names, and yet they've saved me time and time again.

Although she lives the life of a lay monastic, Rosalie doesn't identify with the New Monasticism® movement. Often she is excluded from their events because she is part of the over-forty crowd. Sometimes we've forgotten the wisdom that an old soul can bring into a contemporary conversation, especially when we're talking about a monastic tradition that can be traced back to the third century.

Later that evening, Rosalie and I joined some emerging Episcopalians at a theology pub. For those who think this dialogue is limited to the young adult crew, a good chunk of this crowd was over thirty-five. They seemed attracted to this ongoing conversation of how to breathe life into a seemingly dying institutional church — though since this was a "bluer than blue" state, the conversation kept shifting to politics. Despite my best efforts to keep the discussion on a nonpartisan basis, I let my mouth and the conversation get out of hand a few times.

Going to the Grotto

After paying homage to Powell's Books — a must-see stop on any book lover's pilgrimage — and reflecting in the Portland Classical Chinese Garden, I felt a rather bizarre compulsion to visit The National Sanctuary of Our Sorrowful Mother, The Grotto.

Once I set foot on the pilgrim path of this pine-wooded sixty-two-acre sanctuary, I heard a recording of monks chanting in the background. After a quick stop to reflect at the sculpture of the wounded Christ carrying his cross, I came face-to-face with the sanctuary's central attraction — Our Lady's Grotto. Carved in 1925 from solid basalt in the cliff wall, this stone altar featured a white replica of Michelangelo's *Pieta*. High above this grotto stood a giant bronze statue of Our Sorrowful Mother.

When I entered the elevator that would take me to the upper-level grounds, the chanting stopped. An oddly comforting female voice welcomed me to the next level. Images of the HAL 9000 computer from *2001: A Space Odyssey* started dancing through my head — only this time, Catholics, not computers, have overtaken the world. When I got to the top, I went into a steel spacelike meditation chapel. The lifelike statue of the Virgin Mary and the baby Jesus encased in a glass pod-like structure and the fine leather chairs made me feel like I was in some futuristic facility with no exit, unsure if I should be waiting for Godot or God.

As I passed by the peace pole and walked through the peace garden, I found myself humming "I Think I Love

You." After several attempts to get this Partridge Family bubblegum bunk out of my head, I came close to losing my Christian cookies when that song segued into some CCM-coated version of "I Have Decided to Follow Jesus." Once again, when I'm in a place of sorrow, I tend to break out in a case of the sillies.

I descended down the elevator with my mind filled with God gunk. "Mrs. Hal" thanked me for paying her a visit, but instead of responding in kind, I fled before she could wake her partner, Hal, from his slumber. A meeting with young adults exploring intentional communities helped me regain my spiritual bearings.

Sunday Services Smorgasbord

I started my Sunday at Saints Peter and Paul Church. An Anglo-Celtic vibe lent a traditional yet graceful air to this multiracial gathering. During his sermon on Exodus 10 ("The Locust Nonsense"), Kurt Neilson presented us with two versions of Moses. He started to describe the Hollywood version of this story, in which a chiseled Moses comes out with his mighty staff, when a homeless man walked into the sanctuary aided by his walking stick. If I didn't know better, I would have thought Kurt planted that transition from the glitzy prophet to the cranky Moses who was more mess than majesty. But, as Kurt reminded us, this messiness is where God meets us. And in crankiness, we find community.

At coffee hour, I met a woman who worked for the L'Arche Community in Portland. She brought two guests to church. I was struck by how her strong yet gentle presence enabled two very physically challenged men to participate in the church service and coffee hour. In observing this woman at work, I realized the extent to which I had overromanticized Henri Nouwen's work with this community. His book *The Wounded Healer* saved me years ago, and from time to time I would fanaticize about how someday I would be "good" enough that I could follow in his otherworldly footsteps. The reality staring me straight in the face told me that people with my prickly personality lack the patience to venture down Henri's path.

Instead, I need to keep my focus on climbing those mountains that call my name.

Also, I ran into author and Presbyterian pastor Karen Sloan, who decided to visit as well. We had met briefly in Redmond, where I suggested she might want to connect with my buddy Kurt. After we said our hellos, we noted we'd be seeing each other again in a few minutes at The Bridge. Pam Hogeweide, another kind soul I met in Redmond, offered to serve as my chauffeur and guide for the afternoon.

Ten years ago, Ken and Deborah Loyd formed The Bridge as a way to connect with those Portland-area kids who felt disenfranchised and marginalized from the larger culture. Every Sunday, about seventy-five people come together for what I would describe as a primal drumming ceremony with a definite R&B funk beat. Led by worship leaders Angie and Todd Fadel, some people danced and others stomped their feet, but they all threw themselves into the service until the floor vibrated. After much music, a message, and an interactive writing exercise, many in the congregation moved to the basement for the weekly distribution of groceries. I sensed most traditional churches would show these alleged "hooligans" the door, but at The Bridge they've found a home where they can belong and be loved just as they are.

In 2006, Ken left The Bridge to form HOMEpdx to serve his "friends without homes." This barebones operation works with local churches and individuals who send volunteers and food each Sunday, as well as assisting with other needs. The

Ken Loyd setting out to find people to hang out with, as well as give out burritos and other stuff

lack of a formal infrastructure enables them to address immediate needs quickly when larger, more bureaucratic channels would take too long. Think of HOMEpdx as a speedboat zipping between oil tankers.

By the time Pam and I arrived at their outdoor gathering, a group of church volunteers was already situated under a city bridge and serving a meal. We passed out socks, though I stood more in the background. With her tattoos and street sense, Pam was much better equipped to connect with these guests than I was. As we were leaving, Pam introduced me to Ken Loyd, a white-haired man with a Mohawk, piercings, and plenty of tattoos.

A former welder and fabricator, Ken never studied for the professional ministry. Before coming to Portland, Ken and Deborah were on the staff of a megachurch in Washington State. According to Ken, out of a staff of seventeen, he was number seventeen on the theological totem pole. But that was OK with him. Being a pastor wasn't his end goal. He just saw some people that nobody wanted and found an avenue into their lives that worked. While HOMEpdx folks provide food and some tangible items, Ken seeks opportunities to create situations where they can spend time together with hurting people. If in the process someone comes to Jesus, they're thrilled, but the HOMEpdx team isn't one for tract talk.

When Ken described his ministry to me, I saw how he gives each of these faces a name and lets them know they are loved just as they are.

If you draw a blank circle, that is a homeless person. If you put ears, eyes, nose, and hair on them, then it's a friend who lives outdoors. Once you see the face, it's harder to detest and despise the person. In the church world, we somehow think we came on this salvation thing by some means other than God's grace. When someone doesn't fit our model, we assume we got ours by doing something good and they got theirs by doing something bad.

Technically we're a church. I want people to know they're not just coming for a meal. But I wanted to create a church that's not about you (i.e., middle-class you) but the person we're serving. The gospel is about making us well enough to serve. People deserve to be loved simply because they exist. Ours is an agenda driven by love.

I'd encourage people to see the people of whatever town or city they live in as people. Pay attention to their needs, so you're serving them in such a way that they feel they're served. I chose to work with people without homes because when I am around them, they make my heart sparkle. Find the people that make your heart sparkle — these are the ones you're called to serve.

In today's wobbly economic times, it wouldn't take much to send any of us under the bridge. In fact, I see more than one person standing in line who could have been my father, my mother, or even me. Ken's ministry of presence served as a visible reminder to me of how we need each other now more than ever.

For those who like to paint the face of poverty with a black or brown brush, almost all the folks I saw under that bridge looked pretty white to me. (Notice how all the Katrina coverage was on the African Americans living in New Orleans. They seldom ventured down the bayou to report on the conditions of the Caucasian Cajuns.) The seemingly invisible presence of "poor white folks" remains one of the U.S.'s dirty little secrets. Guess it's easier to deal with poverty when the nameless faces don't have the same features as the vast majority of those in corporate and political power.

My brief time with Ken reminded me again of how often we lose the ability to communicate heart to heart with the other. We can spend so much time donning our armor of God that we forget how to care for the least of these. But once we put down our shields and open our hearts, then, like Ken, maybe we can hear the call of God guiding us.

A drawback of the writer's life is that we're out there butt-nekkid for the world to see and slam. Everything we say and do can become faith fodder for the theological tabloids. (Then again, unless a publisher hog-ties an aspiring writer and forces pen to paper, we choose of our own free will to go public with our prose.)

Still, at times I envy those like Ken who can live an unnoticed life where every act they do can be for the glory of God without being subject to public scrutiny. Such simple actions might not make for the best blog battles. But it's through such ordinariness that Jesus of Nazareth came into this world. Jesus often met just one person at a time — the woman at the well (John 4:1–26), the man cured of leprosy (Mark 1:40–45), or even Saul on the road to Damascus (Acts 9:1–19). These one-on-one encounters with the living Christ transformed the world. I felt my pilgrim's journey had just begun when it was time for me to go. On the plane ride home, the silence was shattered by a shrieking child. At first I wanted to reach out and hug the kid, but when he told his parents to shut up and go to hell (and worse), I decided to sit and chill. Sometimes praying in one's seat is the best move one can make.

A Brief Anglican Interlude

When the Rev. Steve Hollinghurst told me he was coming to New York City, I had a hunch I should connect him with Jeannine Otis, given the fact that he's considered one of the foremost researchers into the UK Anglican post-Christian church scene. I first met Jeannine when I was covering HipHopEMass a number of years ago. While she doesn't self-identify as a member of the emerging church movement, in her roles as worship leader for St. Mark's Church in-the-Bowery and a member of the Standing Commission on Liturgy and Music for the U.S. Episcopal Church, she clearly embodies this global spirit I keep meeting everywhere I go.

During my lunch with Steve, his wife, Anne, and Jeannine, I confess I did a bit more talking than I'd like. Still, I jotted down a few reflections on a napkin, which gave me considerable food for thought.

> **Steve**: How does church happen for people who don't fit into the traditional model of church? I see the value in observing how churches operate in different contexts. But this isn't so church leaders can replicate various models they see in their

own churches. Rather, we need to be in conversation with each other and see what we can learn from each other's experiences.

Jeannine: In the spirit of worship, you are guided by a higher power. I want to organize the service and have it run well. But I know I need to create a space where God can enter. This isn't easy at times. But even if it gets out of line and gets bigger, it has to come back to why you're doing this. We gather together to worship God and to build community.

In her capacity as one of the Residentiary Canons of the Manchester Cathedral, Anne observed how the presence of their new dean from South Africa has drawn ethnic minorities to the cathedral. She reminded me that communities are enriched by having a diversity of voices adding to the conversation.

I'm a satirist, not a social strategist, but our brief time together reflected the stories that Ori Brafman and Rod Beckstrom tell in their book *The Starfish and the Spider*. They contrast a centralized spider model of management (which dies if you cut off one piece of the spider) with the decentralized starfish system (where you can slice the starfish to smithereens and yet it still grows).

In a decentralized organization, there's no clear leader, no hierarchy, and no headquarters. If and when a leader does emerge, that person has little power over others. The best that person can do to influence people is to lead by example.

Lest anyone feel they are promoting lawless leadership, they offer this clarification in their book:

That doesn't mean that a decentralized system is the same as anarchy. There are rules and norms, but these aren't enforced by any one person. Rather, the power is distributed among all the people and across geographic regions.

What I found particularly interesting was their analysis of hybrid organizations, such as eBay, that have a centralized structure but rely on a series of decentralized networks as well. Steve's research demonstrated how the UK Anglican Church employed a similar model by supporting traditional churches (which works well for some people), while encouraging other approaches to reach those who are not likely to set foot inside an Anglican church.

However, I don't see how this starfish stuff can happen as long as we place select leaders on pastoral pedestals as though they represent the ones who will impart all the knowledge to us. Even if those gathered break out into small discussion groups, the expert-led conversations tend to remain focused on the cerebral. Now, I don't want to discount the wisdom I have learned throughout the years by soaking in such academics as N. T. Wright, Harvey Cox, and Jeff Sharlet. Without this solid scholarship, my work would veer off into some feel-good tangents that lack any solid footing whatsoever.

But Jesus taught us through the Last Supper that ultimately our knowing must move from the head and enter our hearts, "for where two or three come together in my name, there am I with them" (Matthew 18:20). Through the intimate act of breaking bread together, we meet the face of the risen Christ and become united as a body of believers. I've lost track of the number of times I've had an intellectual tiff or a personal grudge that dissipated, at least for a bit, when we took Communion together. Sometimes we were ready to reconcile, but all too often, our petty problems resumed shortly after the service was over. Still, there was that moment when I could see at least a glimpse of Christ in the person who was driving me crazy.

Midwest Missions

Onward to Minneapolis, Minnesota, to hang out with my buddy Mark Van Steenwyk, the founder of Missio Dei, an Anabaptist lay

intentional community, and editor of the webzine *The Jesus Manifesto*. I stayed in one of Missio Dei's two houses located in the West Bank of Minneapolis. For two days I participated in its rather informal rule of life. Every morning and evening, those who are around each house gather for prayers, using *The Missio Dei Breviary*. In the evenings, I joined in their communal meals, including the weekly meal where both houses come together. At this gathering, they extended invitations for former members and others in their informal circle to join them for food and fellowship.

The group tended to be fairly young and laid-back. Most of them are from the area, but others in the group had connected virtually with Missio Dei before they came to live with them. If you didn't spot the bits of religious imagery around, you might suspect this was a post-college hangout. In fact, Missio Dei faces zoning hassles from the city of Minneapolis, which treats their homes as rental units. The city operates under the mistaken assumption that Missio Dei is a bunch of roommates when, in fact, it is an independent lay religious community. If Mark were a monk, then Missio Dei would be treated like a proper monastery, though I suspect his wife and son would not be thrilled with this decision.

These Anabaptists tend toward anarchy, though almost all of them voted in the 2008 presidential election. (Mark remained the lone holdout who refused to go to the polls.) He wryly observes, "There isn't even the possibility of political unity among Anabaptists. But once folks understand one another, they can find some ways to work together — or at least not waste so much time being angry toward one another, which is so counterproductive."

Like COTA, The Bridge, and some of the other communities I keep discovering, Missio Dei's work doesn't sparkle as though some theological Tinker Bell dusted the community with faith fairy dust. Instead of engaging in anarchic, and at times asinine, bull sessions, they choose to focus on seeing how they can be present as Christ in the lives of their local community. During my tour of the West Bank area of Minneapolis, I saw the spot where they host a hospitality gathering. Every Saturday, they offer soup and services to all who come. In addition, they volunteer with Cedar Riverside Adult Education Collaborative, which is a literacy program based in one of the nearby apartment complexes that house Minnesota's growing Somali population.

In keeping with the simple rhythm of the community, Mark has an arrangement with his family and community so he is away only five days a month. In addition, Mark surrounds himself with other people he trusts to help him discern if a particular project is helpful to the movement or a vehicle for self-promotion. Sometimes he will take a speaking gig to help finance this work, adding that he's aware of the temptation to become an author/speaker for whom money becomes the driving force in determining where he will go. When possible, he tries to spend his time hanging with other communities so they can learn from each other.

Alas, I missed the Mall of America and other signs of Minnesota's consumerist culture. But I needed to take off for Chicago and attend the annual meeting of the American Academy of Religion (AAR). Just as well, because I doubt Missio Dei does malls.

Obamaland Bound

Nothing like being on Obama's home turf during the week of the 2008 presidential election and sitting in on a daylong seminar on religion and politics with "Obama academics" to send me into a church-state faith frenzy. Fortunately, I was staying with fellow *Door* writer Tamara Jaffe-Notier. This modern-day hippie, who lives in the funky Oak section of Chicago, helped put me in the right frame of mind so I could remain mellow despite this madness.

During AAR, I also reconnected with Craig Detweiler and caught the tail end of his screening for *A Purple State of Mind*. One of Craig's lines from the documentary stayed with me: "Just arguing about God — I don't see it helping anybody." Those of us crammed together in a too-small screening room seemed to agree with his assessment.

I first emailed Helen Mildenhall, the website manager for Off The Map, regarding their work promoting respectful dialogue between Christians and atheists. So I knew of Helen, but I was pleasantly surprised when she stopped by to join my host, Tamara, for Sunday breakfast. Our conversation turned to faith on the fringes, a topic that keeps emerging wherever I go. Surveys tend to box in our beliefs, as though we can fit inside some Christian cubicle. I wonder how many people check off the Christian box even though they're standing on the ledge, wanting to believe but unable to buy into the Jesus junk anymore.

I contemplated attending Obama's former church, but my Anglican sensibilities won out. A friend directed me to Grace Episcopal Church, a church located in Chicago's Printer's Row. The multiple banners welcoming me to Grace Place told me that I was entering not just a church but a community center that also housed the national office for the Episcopal Peace Fellowship, the Great Lakes Regional Office of the American Friends Service Committee, and a not-for-profit consortium of religious communities committed to affordable housing.

Since this was the Sunday before election, I expected a deep-dish serving of Chicago political cheese with a pro-Obama crust. Instead, the rector delivered an All Saints Day message that touched on our tendencies to be bystanders. Using the story of Dietrich Bonhoeffer, he reminded us not to be dulled to the demands of the gospel, for we are agents of God's radical love.

As part of this year's AAR activities, I was asked to join four other authors in leading discussion groups on emerging church as part of a theology pub. Even though this gathering had scant advertising and was held off-site at a pub, the meeting room was packed with over seventy folks (and this doesn't include those who told me they had a conflict that evening). Compare this lively interactive crowd to thirty-some folks who came to see a highly publicized philosophical emergent dialogue. (Ten of them left within the hour with a prunelike look on their faces.) Seems to me that even in an academic environment, an interactive and decentralized format seems to be a more fluid way to move the dialogue forward regarding what it really means to be "the church of the twenty-first century."

Before heading home, I wandered around Grant Park, where already the pre-election crowds were starting to gather. Clearly Obamamania infected this city. It was time for me to leave before I came down with a case of partisanitis.

The Connections Continue

Shortly after I landed back in New York City, I was asked to participate in a postelection discussion hosted by New York Faith & Justice. The diverse panel, consisting of voices ranging from agnostic to moderately conservative, allowed for a broader exchange of ideas and less anti-Republican rantings than what one finds at most progressive forums.

After hearing Jose Humphreys talk about his desire to create an inclusive church, I decided to head over to the National Black Theatre of Harlem and see what was up with Metro Hope Church. I'm not a power-praise charismatic. But this group of about forty faithful welcomed me with arms lifted in the air. Somehow, Jose was able to bring together African-American and Latino Pentecostals with white and Asian charismatics. I missed not partaking in the Eucharist, but at least I was fed coffee and donuts before the service.

On first glance, Jose's "A Tree in Harlem" initiative might appear to be an uptown effort to replant the "A Tree Grows in Brooklyn" phenomenon.  Metro Hope's effort brought together its members who wanted to bring about shalom in their neighborhood. During a prayer-led meeting, they explored what they could do as a church to help combat some of Harlem's key problems, such as the community's high asthma and incarceration rates, as well as its low educational rankings. Jose explains his vision for Metro Hope: "I see us becoming a part of the root system of our neighborhood and city because I believe change happens from the lowliest places. Christ exemplified this when he became flesh and moved into the neighborhood and did the ultimate work with some great friends along the way."

During a visit to Boston, I decided to see what was up with The Crossing. This urban multicultural community based at St. Paul's Cathedral in Boston welcomes people to experience the Groovement, a communal effort to weave the sounds of soul into the Anglican tradition. *The Book of Common Prayer* truly became the prayers of the common people when we all held out our hands to bless the elements. In the paradox of power, by giving up the priestly position in which one person is "in charge," the Rev. Stephanie Spellers has used her skills in community organizing to create a starfish-type Christian community. In this sacred space, all present are called to become sacramental beings equipped to live out the gospel teachings of Christ.

Following The Crossing service, I headed over to the Society of St. John the Evangelist. When I lived in the area during the early 1990s, this monastic community provided a safe haven for me after a rather disastrous falling out with a high-society Boston church. (This was back in the days when I harbored the delusion that I could be a country-club Christian.) Once again, their simple rhythm of life and warm hospitality with communal meals taken in silence, coupled with the lack of Wi-Fi and a ban on cell phone use, afforded me a much-needed opportunity to turn off the outside world and tune in to God. Now that I'm more attuned to the warning signs that all is not well with my soul, I can stop and refocus before I implode.

In watching Jeannine, Jose, and Stephanie in action, I realized that, with the exception of my trips to Israel and Jordan, most of my travels connected me with predominantly white Western European cultures. For all my talk about our need to expand our horizons, I had some major work to do on my end. So I reached out to David

Ramos of the Latino Leadership Circle and the Rev. Gabriel A. Salguero, director of the Hispanic Leadership Program at Princeton Theological Seminary, to start a conversation about how we can connect cross-culturally.

Around this time, Andrew Jones invited me to participate in the Global Roundtable of Underground and Emerging Ministries, an informal network of international ministers. This group met at the Slot Art Festival in Lubiaz, Poland, a gathering of five thousand mostly young-adult Polish Christians. (So much for the myth that Europe has gone totally secular. Also, check out Down Under and elsewhere outside the United States, and often one can find ample signs that the Spirit is alive and kicking if one knows where to look.)

Admittedly, I felt harried, as I was also giving a series of four talks and participating in a panel on global emerging church. Yet, for once, I was able to be still long enough to really hear how God brings Christ-followers together. I learned how Christianity is growing like wildfire in the Global South and Asia. Historically, the West has assumed the role of giver by sending out missionaries to these areas. How will we respond when these missionaries come back to us? The way Christianity gets lived out in these continents looks much different from the empire-based interpretations that have functioned as the dominant narrative since the time of Constantine. Will Westernized Christians be able to assume the role of receiver?

As I continue in my travels, instead of assuming the role of a Western missionary (a position no satirist should fulfill anyway), I'd rather travel as a pilgrim to see what I can learn from other cultures. My initial inquiries tell me there's a growing desire for us to stop exporting our brand of Americana Christianity™, not to mention the misuse of photographs and stories of starving souls as a fund-raising tool. Yes, one does need a personal connection to increase awareness and convince people that this cause justifies their money. But there's a line between generating awareness and capturing "the money shot" — some charities get it; too many end up pushing the equivalent of humanitarian porn by producing eye-catching layouts of "the least of these." On a side note, ever wonder what those people featured in those slick donation brochures are really thinking?

Shannon Hopkins, Brad Sargent, and their crew of merry missionals may be showing us a way forward as they craft a social accounting system to monitor a project's impact to discern if the venture is socially transformative, environmentally responsible, and economically self-sustainable, and if it brings spiritual renewal and reconciliation. To date, Shannon notes that these ventures are often spearheaded in the UK by Christians; here in the States one finds gatherings like The Feast Conference led by humanist collectives. However, I sense a growing receptivity to exploring how U.S. Christians can work alongside those in need through microenterprise business ventures and other cooperative actions so they can achieve self-sufficiency while retaining their indigenous culture.

I share this skepticism about gonzo evangelism. The Big Apple has always been a magnet for those evangelical groups determined to convert the natives. "If you can win a soul here, you can win one anywhere," or so they sing. Every summer, hordes of farm-raised fundies pile into some church-sponsored bus and make a beeline toward this city of sin. After partaking in an all-night pizza party held inside some un-air-conditioned basement, they sashay up and down Broadway with their hair that praises Jesus and matching youth group T-shirts, handing out granola bars and prayer cards. Some days it looks like the Great White Way is fixin' for a revival, courtesy of the cast of *High School Musical: The Homeschooled Version*.

As an unsaved Anglican, I have the dubious distinction of being one of their prime candidates for conversion. Like Catholics, I'm viewed as an icon-worshiping wino — slightly better than pagans and Jews but still headed right straight to h-e-double-toothpicks. I quit wearing my Yale Divinity School–branded gear years ago after I got tired of explaining that my alma mater was, in fact, a "Christian" institution, even though they refused to condemn such worldly notions as evolution, women in the pulpit, and public schooling.

One of the few silver linings to the global financial crisis that hit us all like a tsunami in December 2008 is that these faith follies ran out of funding. Hopefully they will use this downtime to reevaluate what it means to follow Jesus and where these leaders should direct their financial resources. In an increasingly pluralistic society, these misguided moves tend to repel far more people than they attract. Also, the retention rate for such missional endeavors appears to be pretty short-lived. For every new soul they save, another one back-slides — churning never did strike me as particularly Christlike. Still, I feel a bit sorry for the kids, as they are unwitting pawns in this grand missional scheme where the trip organizers must produce evidence they've saved X number of souls in order to convince donors to keep funding this particular faith franchise.

You Go, J-O!

But even in a down economy, some prosperity preachers still nickel-and-dime the masses. Take, for example, "A Night of Hope with Joel & Victoria." When I found out this dynamic duo would be playing in New York City at the brand-new 1.5-billion-dollar Yankee Stadium, I snagged a press pass to this concert. (Sorry, but if you charge admission, I no longer call it a worship service.)

Prior to the show, Joel and Victoria held a fifteen-minute press conference.

Hello, this is Becky Garrison with *Sojourners*. We're here at Yankee Stadium, which isn't that far from Wall Street. What do you want to say to New Yorkers who are going through this current financial crisis?

JOEL: I would say to them probably what I'm going to say to most of the people today. Keep your head up. Keep believing that good things are going to come, that this is a season that we will pass through. Really, don't get negative. Don't get bitter. Don't get discouraged 'cause that just draws in more of that negativity. So I'm going to encourage people that we all go through difficulties. But I think God can bring us out, and he can somehow bring us out better. So just try to inspire them to keep believing.

VICTORIA: (Smiled and sat this Q out.)

No clue where Jesus is, but I suspect he'd rather not play ball tonight.

At showtime there were still well over ten thousand seats available, so they didn't really hit a home run out of this ballpark.

Not to worry. The show proved to be a major sellout. Those of us present were champions of hope, victors not victims. We're believers, not doubters. Guess mentioning the cost of the cross might be too much of a devotional downer.

I confess I'm not a major fan of crusades in general. They just don't speak to me spiritually. Having said that, when I attended the Billy Graham Crusade in Flushing Meadows, I got the sense that I was in the presence of a man of God. But the Osteen-inspired happy-happy-joy-joy multimedia spectacle made me wonder if I was at a worship service or a motivational seminar.

Once the praise music faded away, Joel and Victoria took the stage. After Joel rejoiced how he was finally getting to live his dream of playing in a professional baseball stadium, Joel and Victoria regaled the crowd with a replay of their favorite hits. Most of what I'm hearing seems to be eerily similar to Joel's Madison Square Garden concert that I covered back in 2006. Has their faith not evolved in these ensuing three years? Surely folks as well traveled as the Osteens might have some new stories they can tell, don't you think?

By sheer coincidence, Dan Merchant, the author and director of the documentary *Lord, Save Us from Your Followers,* was sitting right next to me. When I complained I had seen this motivational multimedia show before, this rock-show expert reminded me that "people come to rock shows expecting to hear the hits," citing how the Rolling Stones sing "Satisfaction" at every concert. He added, "Like the Stones, Osteen's 'Night of Hope' hits the same buttons. Charisma, emotion, nostalgia, dramatic staging (gorgeous night, amazing new ballpark), a sense of community — all Osteen is missing are the flash pots and a B-stage in center field."

But when Joel and Victoria welcomed Matt and Laurie Crouch onto the stage, this went from being another glam-and-glitter religious rock show to a prosperity gospel powwow. Behind these mega-million-watt smiles and the hair that praises Jesus lurks a ministry that makes the eighties-era PTL Club seem like *Little House on the Prairie*. I don't recall nearly this much gospel-lite glitter when I caught Billy Graham in action.

Here's where the Osteens really deviate from the Billy Graham Crusade plan. On top of the $15 admission fee, Joel Osteen Ministries passed the bucket "to support future events like this one." Double-dipping like this doesn't sit well with me, especially when the Trinity Broadcasting Network (TBN) will make a small fortune by carrying this spiritual extravaganza live throughout the world via its thirty-three international satellites. Once one calculates how much money they stand to recoup from this broadcast, one has to wonder why they couldn't let people in gratis and then take a freewill offering. If the Dalai Lama and Billy Graham hosted free events that attracted even more followers, why couldn't the Osteens do likewise?

> *I don't get excited by big-name celebrities or big-star communities. I love to see a little group of, say, three to ten people meeting in a house who are really wrestling with the spirit of the place and the mission of their particular context and how they have become a transformational community for the place that they live in.*
>
> **Mark Berry,** Safespace

Then there's the not-so-itty-bitty problem with their charity of choice. Doing food drops in New York City via Feed the Children comes off as a noble gesture (though naming a facility the "Victoria Osteen Abandoned Baby Center" sounds like a real Madonna-like move). But the American Institute of Philanthropy consistently gives this charity an F rating for low program spending and high fund-raising costs.

As I'm watching everyone raise their hands and reach into their wallets, my heart sinks. I know many people flock to Joel because they love his hope-filled message. And yes, we do need people who can present positive images of the faith, given the fact that Christians are often depicted in the media as Fred Phelps and Ann Coulter's love child. But what is Christianity without the cross? Also, I just hate watching people fill up on faith fast food when I know there are so many other healthier charismatic communities where they can raise their hands and really do some good for God.

Meanwhile, some spiritual sparks in New York City started to catch fire. Tiny flickers of God kept popping up all over the place. I began to see more and more Christians seeking ways to live out their faith in communities that maintained a commitment to nurture the inner life as well as to engage the outside world. Across the denominational spectrum, such voices seem to be uniting.

The beauty in pulling people together, as communities do, is this: people are appreciated for the gifts, talents, and callings they bring to the table and there is a holy anarchy to what comes out of those interactions.

Chris Enstad

Back in 2007, I ran into Jason and Vonetta Storbakken, who were just starting Radical Living, an intentional living community in the Bedford-Stuyvesant section of Brooklyn. A former writer for *High Times*, Jason was now seeking ways he could get high on the Holy Spirit. Through Jason, I connected with a range of folks seeking to live in community — from Catholic Workers and Harlem House (the Bruderhof Community) to a few Christians who started off as roommates and wanted to take their living situation to the next level.

As Radical Living continues to grow, they've begun exploring ways to extend their mission by hosting fellow travelers and sponsoring forums and Bible studies on topics like immigration, as well as participating in local community projects and launching a food pantry. Whenever a media outlet reports on these "roommates for Jesus," Jason notes that they will receive a surge of emails from folks asking how they can join the party. He expressed his concern that they might be disappointed if they actually visited the community.

We've had people come from as far away as six hours just to join us for a community dinner. It was a very typical dinner, good company and all, but nothing to come so far for. It goes to show how much people desire to be part of something, particularly community. We used to have a couple of folks wake up at 4:00 a.m. to take the train from Coney Island to join us for our Friday morning prayer and pancakes. We sure liked their company, but it might have been just as good, if not better, if they had opened up their apartment to their friends and neighbors for a prayer breakfast.

When Dave Andrews, an Australian-based Christian community worker and writer, stopped by Radical Living, he shared his grandfatherly wisdom born from a life living in community. Throughout his stories, he emphasized that all he did was try to love those who were deemed unlovable.

We don't invite people to join our community. We invite them to join us. And if we love each other well, community is what happens as result.

Dave Andrews

During Mark Van Steenwyk's stay with Radical Living, we had a chance to reflect on the increasing hunger among Christians throughout the United States to connect to Jesus. There's an acute sense of what doesn't work, coupled with a desire to find new and creative solutions.

Reflections from Mark

Everyone's story is different. Some people come to this point where they feel that Christianity is flimsy. They start talking, but they're not just content to sit around and talk about deconstruction — they want to move toward something meaningful. If you're really looking into

people who have done the Jesus life in the most beautiful and compelling way, it draws you toward looking at different ways of communal expression.

There are also those who went through their Emerging Church phase, who were grateful for being able to deconstruct everything, but then came to realize there was no substance to it. That's my experience, and it drew me into searching for these older stories of substance, which I found in the stories of those living in intentional community.

Mark Van Steenwyk a.k.a. Dave Andrews the Younger

Also, a lot of young people are growing up in churches that think it's trendy to talk about social justice. Because they're young and excited, they take radical justice to its logical conclusion, which is being really connected to a neighborhood, practicing hospitality, and living with other people. They tend to avoid attention and often don't have the money or desire to attend formal gatherings. But if you want to find where the radical movements are, go among the marginal and poor, where injustices are happening. Then see how you can get connected to where God is already at work within this community.

I realized along the way that I quit trying to find Jesus and simply let him do the talking. Every so often, I felt God's presence when walking on soil or I saw God's face in other souls. Other times, I'd feel nothing. But that usually meant I either looked in the wrong place or didn't sit still long enough for God to enter the picture. Now, even when I feel all alone, I no longer think God has abandoned me. (After all, who do I think I am — Mother Teresa?)

In looking over the pictures from my travels, I see I've taken only a small smattering of snapshots. Along with photos of empires that kind of turned my stomach, I also tried to capture those people and places that spoke to my heart. In honesty, I have no idea what these pictures will look like a year from now, though my hope and prayer is that as these seekers wander in the wilderness, they keep traveling forward on their path toward God.

As an Anglican, I connect with Christ through ritual that is grounded in the past but looks to the future. But I fully understand how others can experience God through means that don't speak to me. What if we all took our own cameras and photographed what the body of Christ looks like to each one of us? That would be a slide show worth watching.

I longed for a Christianity that was "evangelical" in the sense of being "good news" to our hurting world that had integrity when it came to the context of the early Christians and how they would have understood the gospel (instead of just arguments of the sixteenth century read back into Scripture). I've become convinced that the gospel is about God's will being done "on earth," as Jesus taught us to pray, and that we don't "go to glory," rather biblically glory is coming here and it has broken in through Jesus!

Jarrod Saul McKenna,
peace-preaching eco-evangelist,
"Wednesdays with Gandhi"

Despite our ecclesiological and theological differences, through the breaking of bread, we become joined together as the body of Christ. For as Jesus said, "This is my body given for you; do this in remembrance of me" (Luke 22:19). As I continue on my journey, I participate in the Last Supper with my fellow believers though a myriad of rituals:

> crypt Communion at Canterbury Cathedral
> evangelical snacks
> ambient chill Eucharist
> high Celtic mass
> meal under the bridge
> passing out snacks in the park
> Communion by numbers
> donuts and coffee before church
> circle celebrations where we administered
>   the Lord's Supper to each other
> people getting groceries after church
> picnic in the park
> community agape fest

Rather than ascertaining if a church is emergent/progressive/ orthodox/mainline — or whatever the label du jour might be — perhaps the question we should ask is this: Is Christ present?

The Promised Land?

We Christians were never the hope. Yes, we were and are carriers of the hope. But we ourselves are only reflections — often dim reflections — of the hope we internalize: Jesus Christ.

Sarah Cunningham, *Dear Church*

In *Surprised by Hope*, N. T. Wright explores how we as Christians can bring hope here on earth.

The kingdom will come as the church, energized by the Spirit, goes out into the world vulnerable, suffering, praising, praying, misunderstood, misjudged, vindicated, celebrating: always — as Paul puts it in one of his letters — bearing in the body the dying of Jesus so that the life of Jesus may also be displayed.

As Christians, we're commanded to be prophetic voices proclaiming this hope. We can so easily join in the faith frenzy as we chase after the next big thing that we end up worshiping the latest American Idol–ized pious pop star instead of following the living Christ. Or when championing some very worthy causes, religious leaders can easily become politicians' biblical buttboys who get trotted out onstage whenever a politico wants to secure the "Christian" vote.

If we choose to put Jesus' teachings into practice, we're going to make waves. Prophets never win popularity contests. Even Jesus got the boot from his hometown (Luke 4:16–30).

To be honest, I have no clue what we're going to find if we set sail and chart our course toward the risen Christ. But then again, neither did Mary Magdalene when she went to the tomb. At least she had the audacity to go inside and proclaim the good news, "I have seen the Lord!" (John 20:18). And the world would never be the same. Let us have the courage to do likewise.

For Further Reading ...
Reflection ... Respite

The Book of Common Prayer (1979), p. 358.

Geez (*www.geezmagazine.org*).

Murray Stiller, quoted in Becky Garrison, "The Spirituality of Spamalot," *The Jesus Manifesto* (*www.jesusmanifesto.com*).

The *Itinerarium*

Mike Yaconelli, *Dangerous Wonder*, p. 24.

Cartoon: "God Blimp," © *www.nakedpastor.com*.

Phil Cousineau, *The Art of Pilgrimage*, pp. xxix–xxx.

Cartoon: "Inclement Weather," © *www.nakedpastor.com*.

Holy Land Happenings

Israel Ministry of Tourism (*www.goisrael.com/tourism_eng*).

The Holy Land Experience (*www.holylandexperience.com*).

Cartoon: © Jack Corbett, originally published in *The Wittenburg Door*.

William Dalrymple, *From the Holy Mountain*, p. 310.

Rob Lacey, "Gethsemane Park," *The Word on the Street* (CD).

Jerome Murphy-O'Connor, *The Holy Land: An Oxford Archaeological Guide*, p. 49.

Becky Garrison, "Coloring outside the Christian Circle," in *Taking Flight*, Wikiklesia: Volume 2.

Karen Spears Zacharias, *Where's Your Jesus Now?* p. 109.

Stephen Colbert, *I Am America (And So Can You)*, p. 46.

Monty Python's Life of Brian (1979).

Ministry of Tourism and Antiquities (*www.visit-palestine.com*).

Evangelical Lutheran Christmas Church (*www. bethlehemchristmaslutheran.org*).

Jonnys in the Basement, "Human," from the album *Backbone* (Proost, UK, *www.proost.co.uk*).

Becky Garrison, "Travel in the Holy Land a No Go," *Killing the Buddha* (*www.killingthebuddha.com*).

Becky Garrison, "A Few Reflections as a First Time Pilgrim," *TheOoze* (*www.theooze.com*).

Cutting the Christian Cheese

Mike Yaconelli, *Messy Spirituality*, pp. 32–33.

Book Expo America (*www.bookexpoamerica.com*).

Cartoon: "Idolatry," © Andy Singer.

William Shakespeare, *Macbeth* (act 2, scene 3).

Kester Brewin, "What Are The 'Grand Challenges' for Theology for the 21st Century?" (*www.kesterbrewin.com*).

Becky Garrison, "What Would Jesus Buy?" God's Politics (*http://blog .beliefnet.com/godspolitics/*).

Tom Sine, *The New Conspirators*, p. 82.

Peter Walker, Emerging Christian (*www.emergingchristian.com*).

Larry Norman, "Elvis Has Left the Building," from the album *A Moment in Time* (1994).

"The Writer," © Nancy Little Garrison.

Walking the Thin Line

Andrew Jones, "Measuring Emergentness by Smilies," Tall Skinny Kiwi (*http://tallskinnykiwi.typepad.com*).

Becky Garrison, "A Mixed Economy of Church in a Post-Christian Marketplace," *Reflections* (Yale Divinity School, Fall 2009).

Visit Britain (*www.visitbritain.com*).

Phyllis Tickle, *The Great Emergence*, p. 121.

Cartoon: "The evolution of a worshipper," © Dave Walker (*www.CartoonChurch.com*).

Jonny Baker (*http://jonnybaker.blogs.com/jonnybaker*).

Steve Collins (*www.btinternet.com/~smallritual*).

Phil Cousineau, *The Art of Pilgrimage*, p. xxiii.

Canterbury Official Tourism Website (*www.canterbury.co.uk*).

Canterbury Cathedral (*www.canterbury-cathedral.org*).

The Anglican Communion Official Website (*http://www .anglicancommunion.org/ministry/theological/resources/church_ history.cfm*).

Ward's Book of Days, December 29, 1170 (*http://www .wardsbookofdays.com/29december.htm*).

Greenbelt UK (*www.greenbelt.org.uk*).

Jon Birch, "The Ongoing Adventures of ASBO Jesus" (*http://asbojesus.wordpress.com*).

My reflections on the UK church scene are based on emails with the Rev. Steve Hollinghurst, researcher in evangelism to post-Christian culture, The Sheffield Centre (*www.churcharmy .org.uk/sheffieldcentre/*).

Fresh Expressions of Church (*www.freshexpressions.org.uk*).

Episcopal Village (*http://episcopalvillage.org*).

mayBe (*www.maybe.org.uk*).

Barbara Brown Taylor, *An Altar in the World*, p. 62.

Church Mission Society (*www.cms-uk.org*).

Discover Ireland (*www.discoverireland.com*).

Solas Bhride (*www.solasbhride.ie*).

"Favorite Monks: St. Kevin of Glendalough," *The Prayer Foundation* (*http://prayerfoundation.org/favoritemonks/favorite_monks_kevin_ of_glendalough.htm*).

Solas Bhride (*www.solasbhride.ie*).

Visit Dublin (*www.visitdublin.com*).

St. Patrick's Cathedral (*www.stpatrickscathedral.ie*).

Grace (*www.freshworship.org*).

Tower of London (*www.hrp.org.uk/TowerOfLondon*).

Spamalot (2005).

William Shakespeare, *Macbeth* (act 5, scene 1).

Church on the Corner (*www.churchonthecorner.org.uk*).

Balaam's Ass Rides Again

Visit Jordan (*www.visitjordan.com*).

Jordan: Touristic Sites (*http://www.kinghussein.gov.jo/tourism.html*).

Habitat for Humanity Jordan (*http://www.habitat.org/intl/ame/*104.
aspx).

"Dozens held over Jordan bombings," *BBC News*, November 11,
2005 (*http://news.bbc.co.uk/2/hi/middle_east/*4428204.*stm*).

Qur'an Browser (*www.quranbrowser.org*), translation by Khalifa.

Tony Campolo and Mary Darling, *The God of Intimacy and Action*,
p. 34.

Noor Al-Hussein Foundation (*www.nooralhusseinfoundation.org*).

Jason Boyett, *The Pocket Guide to the Bible*, p. 174.

Shane Claiborne, "The Conspiracy of Hope," *Conspire* (Spring
2009).

Becky Garrison, "The Lord of the Flies," *TheOoze* (*www.theooze.com*).

A Divine Nobody Meets the Wright Stuff

John La Grou, "Surfing the Liminal Domains," foreword in *Voices of
the Virtual World*, Wikiklesia: Volume 1, p. 20.

Cartoon: "Emerging church bloggers," © Dave Walker (*www.Cartoon
Church.com*).

Soularize 2007 (*www.soularize.net*).

Blazing Saddles (1974).

Becky Garrison, "Finding the Furious Longing of God," The High Calling (*www.thehighcalling.org*).

Brennan Manning, *The Furious Longing of God*, p. 60.

Jim Palmer (*www.divinenobodies.com/blog*).

Center for Action and Contemplation (*www.cacradicalgrace.org*).

Cashing In at the Christian Casinos

American Academy of Religion (*www.aarweb.com*).

Brad Sargent (*http://futuristguy.wordpress.com*).

Andrew Jones email (2008).

Cartoon: "Just hangin'," © *www.nakedpastor.com*.

Bill Kinnon (*www.kinnon.tv*).

National Cursillo Center (*www.natl-cursillo.org*).

Diana Butler Bass, *Christianity for the Rest of Us*, p. 72.

Andrew Jones, "Emergent Church Difficulties and Differences," Tall Skinny Kiwi (*http://tallskinnykiwi.typepad.com*).

Becky Garrison, "Reports of the Death of the Episcopal Church Are Greatly Exaggerated," *Religion Dispatches* (*www.religiondispatches.org*).

The Barna Group, "Christianity Is No Longer Americans' Default Faith," January 12, 2009.

Harvey Cox, *The Future of Faith*, p. 177.

Rob Lacey, "Shelves of Rule Books," *The Word on the Street* (CD).

Cartoon: "Innovation," © *www.nakedpastor.com*.

Brian Walsh and Sylvia Keesmaat, *Colossians Remixed*.

Becky Garrison, "And They Laid Him in a Manger, Somewhere Out by John Wayne Airport," *The Wittenburg Door* (*www.wittenburgdoor.com*).

San Diego Natural History Museum (*www.sdnhm.org*).

L. William Countryman, *Living on the Border of the Holy*, p. 25.

Becky Garrison, "An Accidental Pilgrimage," *TheOoze* (*www.theooze.com*).

Mother Teresa Unplugged

Alternatives for Simple Living (*www.simpleliving.org*).

Mother Teresa, *Come Be My Light*, pp. 163, 212.

Cartoon 543: © Jon Birch, "The Ongoing Adventures of ASBO Jesus."

Thomas Merton, *Thoughts in Solitude*, p. 79.

Becky Garrison, "Mother Teresa's Advent Light," God's Politics (*http://blog.beliefnet.com/godspolitics/*).

Becky Garrison, "I Am Legend, Isolated but Not Alone," God's Politics (*http://blog.beliefnet.com/godspolitics/*).

Good without God

Purple State of Mind (*http://purplestateofmind.com*).

Cartoon: "The Doomsayers," © April Pederson, originally published in *The Wittenburg Door*.

Greg Epstein (*http://harvardhumanist.org*), *Call + Response* (*www.callandresponse.com*).

Not for Sale Campaign (*www.notforsalecampaign.org*).

Henri Nouwen, *The Life of the Beloved*, p. 118.

Becky Garrison, "Struggling with A *Purple State of Mind*," God's Politics (*http://blog.beliefnet.com/godspolitics/*).

Holy Hippies

Email correspondence with an anonymous former parishioner from St. Bartholomew's Church, Hartsville, South Carolina (Winter 2008).

Photo of the Rev. Karl C. Garrison Jr. provided by Holly Westcott.

Cartoon: "Hippie, Holy Daze," © Andy Singer, originally published in *The Wittenburg Door*.

Don Lattin, *The Harvard Psychedelic Club*, p. 215.

Merrill Markoe, "Enough about You: My Explanation of Narcissism" (*www.merrillmarkoe.com*).

Karl Claudius Garrison Jr., "The Tyranny of Freedom: A Study of Dimensions of the Sacred in the Development of an Activist Sectarian Enterprise" (abstract, 1968).

Email correspondence with Kurt Neilson (Winter 2008).

Photo of Davidson College protest, 1970, courtesy of Davidson College archives.

Margaret Feinberg, *The Sacred Echo*, p. 169.

Karl Barth, *Fragments Grave and Gay*, p. 124.

The More Things Change ...

Becky Garrison, "The Pope vs. Spiderman," *The Wittenburg Door* (*www.wittenburgdoor.com*).

Deep Shift (*www.deepshift.org*).

Cartoon: "Lil Yacs," © Dan Foote, originally published in *The Wittenburg Door*.

Mike Yaconelli memorial (*www.youthspecialties.com/yaconelli/words*).

Cartoon: "God's quotable quotes," © *www.nakedpastor.com*.

Steve Taylor (*www.emergentkiwi.org.nz*).

Robert Darden, *Jesus Laughed*, p. 47.

Becky Garrison, "Taking Steps toward Forgiveness," The High Calling (*www.thehighcalling.org*).

Remembering Rightly

Brooklyn Wall of Remembrance (*www.brooklynwall.org*).

Jesus Sent Joe

Cathleen Falsani, *Sin Boldly*, p. 98.

Cartoon 687: © Jon Birch, "The Ongoing Adventures of ASBO Jesus."

All Angels Church (*www.allangelschurch.com*).

Becky Garrison, "Strait Jacket Needed in Assisi," *The Wittenburg Door* (*www.wittenburgdoor.com*).

Paul Moses, *The Saint and the Sultan*, p. 235.

James Martin, SJ, *My Life with the Saints*, p. 278.

The Book of Common Prayer, p. 833.

Rogue Relative

"Cartoon 695," © Jon Birch, "The Ongoing Adventures of ASBO Jesus."

John Winthrop, "City on a Hill" (1630).

Rob Boston, "The Forgotten Founder" (*www.au.org*).

Martha Nussbaum, *Liberty of Conscience*, p. 65.

Bill Leonard, "Conscience and Dissent in a Believers' Church: Renewing Baptists' Global Identity" (speech at Campbellsville University conference, April 2, 2009).

Roger Williams, *The Bloudy Tenent of Persecution for Cause of Conscience* (1644).

Go Newport (*www.gonewport.com*).

"For What It's Worth," lyrics by Stephen Sills, performed by Buffalo Springfield (1967).

Becky Garrison, "Defending Roger," *TheOoze* (*www.theOoze.com*).

Becky Garrison, "Uncovering Your Past to Discover Your Calling," The High Calling (*www.thehighcalling.org*).

When the Saints Go Marching In

Dan Kimball, *They Love Jesus but Not the Church*, p. 78.

Jeff Sharlet, *The Family*.

Frank Schaeffer, "An Open Letter to the 'Respectable' Evangelical/ Republican Party Leadership" (*www.frank-schaeffer.blogspot.com*).

Clergy for Obama (*http://clergy4obama.wordpress.com*).

The Matthew 25 Network (*http://matthew25.org*).

Brennan Manning, *Abba's Child*, p. 74.

Cartoon: "Hunting," © *www.nakedpastor.com*.

Shane Claiborne, *Jesus for President* (*www.jesusforpresident.org*).

Nathan Diebenow email (2008).

Becky Garrison, "Jesus for President: Declaring Independence from Partisan Politics," God's Politics (*http://blog.beliefnet.com/ godspolitics/*).

The Missio Dei Breviary, p. 126.

Living on a Prayer

Metropolitan Museum of Art (*www.metmuseum.org*).

Before the Music Dies (documentary film, 2006).

Yale Divinity School (*www.yale.edu/divinity*).

Gary Austin (*www.garyaustin.net*).

Hugh MacLoed, "Ignore Everybody" (*http://gapingvoid.com*).

Jonny Baker, "The Gift of Not Fitting In" (*http://jonnybaker.blogs .com/jonnybaker*).

The Ordinary Radicals

Becky Garrison, "*The Wittenburg Door* Interview: Phyllis Tickle" (*www.wittenburgdoor.com/phyllis-tickle*).

The Ordinary Radicals (documentary film, 2008) (*www. theordinaryradicals.com*).

Anne Lamott, *Bird by Bird*, p. 124.

C. S. Lewis, *The Screwtape Letters*.

Jason and Vonetta Storbakken, "Reconciliation's Challenge for New Monastic Communities," God's Politics (*http://blog.beliefnet.com/ godspolitics/*).

Go West, Young Man

Church of the Apostles (*www.apostleschurch.org*).

Fremont, Center of the Known Universe (*www.fremontseattle.com*).

Becky Garrison, *Rising from the Ashes: Rethinking Church*, p. 147.

Mustard Seed Associates (*www.msainfo.org*).

Martha Grace Reese (*www.gracenet.info*).

Mars Hill Church (*www.marshillchurch.org*).

"It's All About Jesus: Mars Hill Annual Report (July 1, 2008–June 30, 2009).

For more information on "muscular Christianity," see Jeff Sharlet, *The Family*.

Visit Seattle (*www.visitseattle.org*).

Andrew Jones, "Recession: The Carnival Is Over," Tall Skinny Kiwi (*http://tallskinnykiwi.typepad.com*).

Shannon Hopkins (*http://shannonhopkins.com*).

The Porpoise Diving Life (*www.billdahl.net*).

Becky Garrison, "Which Jesus? The Hope (and Horror) of Religion and Politics," God's Politics (*http://blog.beliefnet.com/godspolitics/*).

Cartoon 541, © Jon Birch, "The Ongoing Adventures of ABSO Jesus."

Saints Peter and Paul Episcopal Church (*www.seekhere.org*).

Becky Garrison, "Celtic Hospitality in the Workplace," The High Calling (*www.thehighcalling.org*).

Mark Pierson (*http://markpierson.org.nz*).

Becky Garrison, "Transitioning into a Ministry of Presence," The High Calling (*www.thehighcalling.org*).

Quaker Abbey (*www.quakerabbey.org*).

Travel Portland (*www.travelportland.com*).

The National Sanctuary of Our Sorrowful Mother, The Grotto (*www.thegrotto.org*).

The Bridge (*http://thebridgeportland.org*).

HOMEpdx (*www.homepdx.net*).

Photo of Ken Loyd taken by Donna Van Horn and used with permission by Ken Loyd.

Steve Hollinghurst (*www.onearthasinheaven.blogspot.com*).

Jahneen (Jeannine) Otis (*www.jahneen.com*).

Ori Brafman and Rod Beckstrom, *The Spider and the Starfish,* pp. 19–20.

American Academy of Religion (*www.aarweb.org*).

Grace Place (*http://gracechicago.org*).

Choose Chicago (*www.choosechicago.com*).

The Connections Continue

New York Faith & Justice (*www.nyfaithjustice.org*).

Metro Hope Church (*http://metrohopenyc.org*).

The Crossing (*www.thecrossingboston.org*).

Society of St. John the Evangelist (*www.ssje.org*).

Slot Art Festival (*www.slot.art.pl*).

Becky Garrison, "Who Will Save Manhattan?" *Killing the Buddha* (*www.killingthebuddha.com*).

Becky Garrison, "Media Fails to Report on Joel Osteen's Unsavory Choice of Charity," *Religion Dispatches,* May 1, 2009 (*www.religiondispatches.org*).

Becky Garrison, "You Go J-O!" God's Politics (*http://blog.beliefnet.com/godspolitics/*).

Dan Merchant, *Lord, Save Us from Your Followers* (documentary film, 2008).

Chris Enstad (*www.livingtheresurrection.typepad.com*).

Safe Space (*http://homepage.mac.com/markjohnberry/safe-space/index.html*).

Radical Living (*http://radicalliving.wordpress.com*).

Joseph Huff-Hannon, "Roommates for Jesus," *New York Press,* July 23, 2008 (*www.nypresss.com*).

Dave Andrews (*www.daveandrews.com.au*).

Mark Van Steenwyk interview (2008).

Jarrod Saul McKenna email (*http://paceebene.org/blog/jarrod-mckenna*).

Epilogue: The Promised Land?

Sarah Cunningham, *Dear Church*, p. 199.

N. T. Wright, *Surprised by Hope*, p. 112.

The Words of Jesus: A Gospel of the Sayings of Our Lord with Reflections by Phyllis Tickle, p. 100.

Acknowledgments

This list remains a work in progress, but here are some of the people who made this project possible ...

Agnes, Alec, Amey, Andrew J., Andrew M., Andrzej, Angela G., Angela S., Beth, Betsy, Bev, Bill D., Bill W., Bob, Bonnie, Brad H., Brad S., Brian M., Brick, Bud, Carl, Chris, Christine, Cindy, Craig, Curt, Cynthia, Dan, Daniel, Dave B., Dave K., Dave S., David K., David R., Diana, Dick, Dirk, Don, Donna, Ed C., Ed V., Edward T., Eleni, Evan, Frank, Gabriel, Gareth, Gary A., Gary G., Giles, Greg, Harmony, Holly, Ian, Jackie, James, Jamie, Jarrod, Jason B., Jason S., Jeannine, Jeff, Jim, Jo, Joan, John A., John B., John H., John L., John and Denise, Jon, Jonny, Joyce, Judy, Julie P., Karen C., Karen W., Kari, Karla, Kathleen, Kelly, Kevin, Kurt, Kyle, Lauren, Linnea C., Linnea G., Liz, Lydia, Marcia, Marcus, Mark F., Mark S., Mark V., Marla, Martha, Matthew, Michael, Mike, Mitri, Murray, Musette, Nancy, Nathan, Paige, Pam, Pat, Phyllis, Priscilla, Rebecca, Roger, Roy, Ruby, Ryan B., Ryan P., Sally, Sam, Shane, Shannon, Spencer, Steve C., Steve H., Susan, Tamara, Tammy, Tim, Tom, Wenndy.

Share Your Thoughts

With the Author: Your comments will be forwarded to the author when you send them to *zauthor@zondervan.com.*

With Zondervan: Submit your review of this book by writing to *zreview@zondervan.com.*

Free Online Resources at
www.zondervan.com

Zondervan AuthorTracker: Be notified whenever your favorite authors publish new books, go on tour, or post an update about what's happening in their lives at www.zondervan.com/authortracker.

Daily Bible Verses and Devotions: Enrich your life with daily Bible verses or devotions that help you start every morning focused on God. Visit www.zondervan.com/newsletters.

Free Email Publications: Sign up for newsletters on Christian living, academic resources, church ministry, fiction, children's resources, and more. Visit www.zondervan.com/newsletters.

Zondervan Bible Search: Find and compare Bible passages in a variety of translations at www.zondervanbiblesearch.com.

Other Benefits: Register yourself to receive online benefits like coupons and special offers, or to participate in research.

ZONDERVAN.com/
AUTHORTRACKER
follow your favorite authors